LOST

IN THE AMAZON

By TOD OLSON

LOST IN THE PACIFIC, 1942

LOST IN OUTER SPACE

LOST IN THE AMAZON

L✺ST

IN THE AMAZON

A BATTLE FOR SURVIVAL in the HEART of the RAINFOREST

TOD OLSON

Scholastic Inc.

Library of Congress Cataloging-in-Publication Data available

ISBN 978-0-545-92827-4

9 2020

Printed in the U.S.A.   23
First edition, February 2018

Book design by Baily Crawford

For Zoë

TABLE OF CONTENTS

DECEMBER 24, 1971

I t was Christmas Eve day, and the terminal at Jorge Chávez International Airport teemed with people, vying for position. Bags full of presents, wrapped and unwrapped, crowded the floor. It seemed like half the population of Lima, Peru, wanted to get home for the holiday—and at least some of them weren't going to make it.

LANSA Airlines had canceled its flight to Cuzco, on the edge of the Andes Mountains. The plane had been delayed for repairs. Only Flight 508 would operate today, the airline announced. It would leave at 11:30 a.m. for Pucallpa and Iquitos, in the heart of the Amazon rainforest.

Dozens of frustrated passengers jostled in line at the airline counter, insisting that the plane take them to Cuzco. The German movie director Werner Herzog elbowed his way forward and made his case. He was desperate to get back to the mountains, where he was shooting a film about a Spanish conquistador who led a disastrous expedition through the jungle more than 400 years ago. Herzog had even bribed LANSA employees with a $20 bill to guarantee him a seat. But now, they said, there was nothing they could do.

Mingling in the crowd were the 86 lucky people who had seats on Flight 508. Maybe they were going to make it home after all.

But while Herzog and others pleaded for a flight out of Lima, at least some of the passengers on Flight 508 were dreading the trip. LANSA had a terrible reputation for safety. Two of its flights had crashed in the last five years; 135 passengers and 13 crew members had boarded a LANSA plane and never gotten off. The last crash had happened just 16 months earlier in Cuzco. LANSA Flight 502 to Lima had 49 exchange students from the United States aboard, fresh from a trek to the ancient Incan city of Machu Picchu. An engine caught fire during takeoff, and the plane careened into a mountainside less than 2 miles from the airport. Only the copilot survived.

The accidents had left LANSA with just a single plane, an old Lockheed L-188 Electra. The plane's wings carried four giant turboprop engines. When the Electra was first made, the engines had a tendency to vibrate so violently they would tear the wings off the fuselage. *LANSA se lanza de panza*, went the saying: "LANSA lands on its belly."

They might joke, but few Peruvians got on a LANSA flight without a shudder of fear. José Guerrero Rovalino was feeling it. He had flown in from Iquitos for his job as an accountant.

American students board the doomed LANSA flight in Cuzco in August 1970.

During the few hours he spent in Lima, he told his mother he didn't trust LANSA to get him back safely.

Narda Sales Rios, a singer, was nervous too. She had tried to change her flight at the last minute, but everything else was booked. Her sister was getting married over the holidays, and she needed to get to Pucallpa for the wedding. She waited anxiously in the terminal with her five-year-old son, Gerard, and a wedding bouquet she had bought for her sister.

Alberto Lozano, a college student, had a friend's warning in the back of his mind. His roommate had come into Lima on a shaky LANSA flight two days before and told Alberto not to risk it. "Don't fly LANSA, brother," the roommate said.

3

"That plane is in bad shape." Alberto shrugged him off. He wanted to get home to spend Christmas with his parents. Besides, he said, he had booked a seat in the tail of the plane, and that was the safest place you could be.

———◦———

At least one passenger wasn't worried at all. Juliane Koepcke approached flying the way she did the rest of life, quietly optimistic and ready for anything. A few weeks earlier, her high school graduating class had flown to Cuzco to explore Machu Picchu, like the exchange students on Flight 502. On the way back, the plane hit a pocket of turbulence and bucked like a wild bull. Most of the class was terrified. Juliane thought the ride was fun.

Then again, at seventeen, Juliane was no stranger to adventure. Her parents were both zoologists. They had come to Peru from Germany to study the plants and animals of the rainforest, and Juliane had spent her childhood following them through the mountains and the jungle. Her city friends might have to deal with a cockroach or a rat every now and then. Juliane had grown up dodging poisonous snakes, alligators, and vampire bats.

For two years she had lived at Panguana, the family's research station deep in the rainforest. During the rainy season, she and her parents could only get there by boat. Their hut stood on stilts to keep it dry when the river flooded. Tarantulas and lizards dropped from the palm-frond roof. Every morning, Juliane

4

had to shake out her boots to make sure no poisonous spiders had moved in during the night.

Now she split her time between Lima and Panguana, city and jungle. It was a strange existence that set her apart from her city friends. Since the age of five she'd been referring to animals by their Latin names. She had raised fig parrots by chewing up bananas and feeding the mush to them. She could imitate the ominous hissing sound of a tarantula. When she came back to Lima after a stay in Panguana, her friends told her she walked strangely. She'd gotten used to lifting her feet high off the ground to keep from tripping over roots.

Over the years, Juliane had been recording bird calls or collecting insects during a lot of important social events. Had it been up to her mother alone, she would have missed the most important one of all. Her graduation from Lima's Alexander von Humboldt school fell on December 23. The night before was the *Fiesta de Promoción*, Peru's version of a senior prom.

Juliane's mother, Maria Koepcke, had wanted Juliane to skip both events. She was anxious to get out of Lima. Juliane's father was waiting for them at Panguana. He had already cut down a Christmas tree and put it up in one of the huts. And Faucett, the more reliable of the two airlines flying to Pucallpa, had no seats on December 24.

The last thing Juliane's mother wanted was to fly LANSA. She had once been on a plane in the United States that had to make an emergency landing with a failing engine. The experience made her skittish every time she flew. Besides, as an ornithologist, she had spent her life studying birds. With their hollow bones, sail-like feathers, and inexhaustible energy, birds were made for flight. A plane, by contrast, was a bulky mass of metal that looked like it should never leave the ground. Maria Koepcke couldn't help feeling that humans weren't meant to fly.

Still, Juliane stood her ground. She loved the rainforest and rarely complained when her parents' work took her away from her friends. But she didn't want to miss graduation. She had saved her money for a long dress with a pretty blue pattern and short sleeves cinched at the end. A college student she'd known for a month, tall and broad shouldered, was taking her to the dance. It would be the last chance she got to say goodbye to many of her friends.

In the end, Maria gave in and bought LANSA tickets. Juliane went to the dance and the next day crossed the stage to receive her diploma.

The following morning, on Christmas Eve, Maria and Juliane stood in line for Flight 508. Out the plate-glass window of the airport, they could see the L-188 Electra that would take them to Pucallpa. To Juliane, the plane looked beautiful, clean and shiny.

It did, however, have an unfortunate nickname. LANSA had stamped the name MATEO PUMACAHUA on the side of the airliner. Pumacahua, as everyone learned in school, had led an

The L-188 Electra had a history of problems with its propellers and wings.

army of indigenous people in rebellion against Peru's Spanish rulers in the early 1800s. His rebels carried slings and clubs into battle against Spaniards armed with rifles. The war did not end well for the rebels, and when it was over, the Spanish authorities hanged Pumacahua for treason. Then they cut him into pieces and sent assorted body parts around the country to be displayed as a warning.

Two young Americans in line next to Juliane noticed the nickname too. Nathan Lyon and David Ericson lived with a group of religious missionaries in the rainforest, not far from the Koepckes' research station. Nathan was just thirteen, but he was determined that sometime in the future he would ride his bike from the rainforest across the mountains to Lima. He had traveled by truck to scout the route and was flying back home to his parents at the missionary community. At eighteen, David had delayed college for a year to help the missionaries provide medical aid and other services to indigenous villages in the area.

Looking out at the plane, Juliane, Nathan, and David saw the opportunity for some dark humor. *Let's hope* this *Mateo Pumacahua keeps its parts intact*, they joked.

———◦———

At around 11 a.m., 86 passengers climbed aboard the LANSA plane. Juliane and her mother, David and Nathan, Narda Sales Rios and her son all took their seats, eager to be home for Christmas. Werner Herzog and his camera crew stayed behind, resigned to another day of waiting.

Juliane found her place next to the window in the second-to-last row, somewhere near the college student Alberto Lozano. Her mother sat to her left in the middle, and a heavyset man settled his bulk into the aisle seat.

At 11:38 a.m., the plane rumbled down the runway with none of the grace of Maria's birds. Its four propeller engines, spinning in a blur, somehow lifted more than 40 tons of metal, baggage, fuel, and passengers into the air. The pilot, Carlos Forno Valera, banked over the Pacific Ocean and headed east toward the Andes Mountains.

The plane was about to carry its passengers through one of the most abrupt transitions a traveler can make on Earth. Lima sits just north of the Atacama Desert, the driest place on the planet. In the Atacama you can find places that don't see rain for four years at a time. Just over the mountains lies the vast expanse of the Amazon rainforest. In the Amazon's northwest corner, where moisture gets trapped against the Andes, 20 feet of precipitation can fall in a single year.

As they climbed toward the crest of the Andes, the cabin was in a holiday mood. Passengers slept, read, or chatted with one another about Christmas plans. Juliane thought the flight attendants seemed cheerful as they served sandwiches and soft drinks.

About 20 minutes into the flight, the plane began to leave the desert air of the coast behind. At 12:09 p.m., Captain Forno Valera radioed in their position over the town of Oyon, nestled in the heart of the Andes at 12,000 feet. He couldn't yet see what awaited them on the other side of the mountain range.

Just 100 miles south and east of Flight 508, a giant mass of moisture-laden air had gathered over the western edge of the rainforest. Trapped against the towering walls of the Andes, the storm rumbled its way northward.

At about 12:20 p.m., the Electra rumbled out of the mountains. Some 20,000 feet below lay the eastern edge of the largest rainforest in the world. But the ground had vanished from view.

The storm, sweeping up from the south, had begun to engulf the route to Pucallpa. The plane had 150 miles to go on a northeast path—a half hour of flying time at the most.

As a thick bank of clouds closed in, Captain Forno Valera faced a choice. He had fuel for four hours total; he could veer north and try to stay ahead of the storm. He could land in Huanuco, which lay almost directly below, and wait out the weather there. He could reverse course and bring everyone back to Lima.

But LANSA had already created dozens of irate customers, stranding them for the holidays when they wanted to be with family. And for all the rain that falls in the Amazon, most storms don't pack a lot of energy. Pilots tried to avoid them,

but when they had to fly in bad weather, they knew what to do: Keep the altitude setting constant, at a safe distance from the ground; don't fight the winds because it puts too much stress on the plane.

Captain Forno Valera set the altitude for 21,000 feet, kept the plane on its northeast route, and pressed ahead.

Out her window on the right side of the plane, Juliane Koepcke could see two of the four big turboprop engines working hard against the heavy air. It wasn't long before the plane began to shudder. The flight attendants made their way through the aisle, telling everyone to fasten their seat belts. To Juliane, it seemed no worse than the flight from Cuzco with her graduating class. But in the middle seat, Maria

was getting anxious. "Hopefully everything will be okay," she said.

The man in the aisle seat slept, oblivious to it all.

The sky outside darkened, as though the pilot had found the mouth of a cave and dived inside. Raindrops pelted the metal sides of the plane. Water streaked the window next to Juliane's face. And now, the shaking turned violent.

The plane lurched up, down, and up again. Water and soda went airborne. Overhead compartments popped open one by one. Flower bouquets, Christmas cakes, and hand luggage flew through the aisle. Lightning bolts pierced the darkness outside, and screams began to fill the cabin.

It got worse by the minute—the vicious shaking, everything coming unmoored in the cabin, the pitch-black sky broken by blinding flashes closer and closer to the plane. Juliane found herself holding hands with her mother. And still the man on the aisle slept.

Twenty minutes into the heart of the storm, the sky outside Juliane's window exploded with lightning. Bright yellow flames erupted from the wing. The plane pitched downward, and before the roar of the engines blocked everything out, Juliane heard her mother say, "It's all over now."

Then she felt a *whoosh* sweep through the plane, and suddenly everything had vanished. She was in the air, strapped to her seat, and all of it was gone—her mother and the sleeping guy and the two boys from the missionary station and the

Seventeen-year-old Juliane Koepcke.

smiling flight attendants and the Christmas presents and the plane.

Even the plane was gone.

The forest below looked to her like densely packed heads of broccoli. And it was spinning slowly and growing closer by the second.

CHAPTER 1

THE GREEN HELL

From the air, the Amazon rainforest looks as though it goes on forever. Move it 2,500 miles north, and you'd have a dense carpet of treetops—400 billion of them—stretching almost unbroken from New York to Florida and from the Atlantic Ocean all the way west to Utah: two-thirds of the continental United States covered in forest. An English naturalist named Richard Spruce came to the Amazon in 1849 to collect plants, insects, and animals and send them back to Europe for museumgoers to gawk at. Just the thought of how vast it was left him breathless. "The largest river in the world flows through the largest forest. Fancy if you can *two millions of square miles of forest*, uninterrupted save by the streams that traverse it."

Europeans first encountered this giant wilderness 470 years before LANSA Flight 508 tried to fly over it. The Amazon had been supporting indigenous communities—"Indians," the newcomers called them—for at least 11,000 years. But to the Europeans it was brand-new.

The Amazon, the dark part at the top of the map, covers an area two-thirds the size of the United States.

They were both fascinated and terrified. "Of all the marvels of nature," wrote the 20th-century explorer Gene Savoy, "the jungle has the power to evoke both fear and wonder in man."

Fear, wonder, and an urge to exaggerate.

A slave trader named Francesco Carletti went to Peru in 1594 and came back with a bizarre description of the rainforest. There were frogs and toads of "frightening size," he claimed, so many of them that people think "they rain down from the sky." Bloodsucking creatures of all kinds preyed on human flesh—from vampire bats to insects that grew fat on blood. "Mandril cats" crossed rivers by linking "themselves together by their tails" and swinging from trees to the other side.

Later reports warned about all the ways a human could be eaten alive in the Amazon. Alligators with an "insatiable desire" for human flesh lurked on every riverbank, according to the Spanish naturalists Jorge Juan and Antonio de Ulloa. A man-eating snake the Indians called *jacumama* lay in wait on the forest floor, disguised as rotten wood. "It will swallow any beast whole, and . . . this has been the miserable end of many a man," wrote Juan and Ulloa. Or so they had heard.

Europeans were just as suspicious of the people who lived in the rainforest, and fear made their imaginations run wild. Explorers returned from South America with fantastical stories about giants, dwarfs, and people whose feet grew backward—the better to confuse anyone who tried to follow their footprints. A tribe of headless men was said to live in the region of Guayana,

How the natives of the New World killed alligators, according to a 16th-century engraving by Theodore de Bry, who had never set foot in the Americas.

on the northern edge of the Amazon. According to the English explorer Sir Walter Raleigh, they had "eyes in their shoulders and their mouths in the middle of their breasts."

Another common story involved a fierce tribe of warrior women. The Spanish explorer Francisco de Orellana supposedly ran across them in 1542 as he traveled from one end of the rainforest to the other. These women towered over everyone and fought as effectively as ten Indian men. They reminded the Spaniards of a group of women warriors from Greek mythology, known as the Amazons. From then on, Europeans had a name for the 4,000-mile-long river that formed the backbone of the forest.

The headless men of Guayana, as depicted in a 1599 book about Sir Walter Raleigh's journey to South America.

But if the rainforest instilled fear in Europeans, it also inspired another powerful urge: greed. In the 1530s, the Spanish conquistador Francisco Pizarro invaded the vast empire of the Incas in the Andes, just on the western edge of the Amazon. He tricked the Inca emperor, Atahualpa, into handing over several tons of gold and silver. Then he had Atahualpa strangled to death in a city square.

The brutal conquest of the Incas gave the indigenous people of the region their first glimpse of guns and cannon fire. But the Spaniards brought a weapon that would prove even more deadly over the next decades: smallpox. The disease was new to the Americas, and native Amazonians had no resistance to it. In the next century, smallpox would play a large part in wiping out nearly 90 percent of the rainforest's indigenous population.

In the meantime, Pizarro's conquest unleashed a craving for gold. When news of Atahualpa's treasure got out, European adventurers started to dream: *Why couldn't there be another empire, as rich as the Incas', lost in the depths of the rainforest?*

Spaniards began to tell a story picked up from Indians around the city of Quito, in present-day Ecuador. According to the legend, buried in the jungle was a kingdom so wealthy that its lord "goes about continually covered in gold dust as fine as ground salt." Every night, the Great Lord washed the gold off in a lake. Every morning he woke up and powdered himself again. In Spanish accounts of the story, the king became known as the Golden One, or El Dorado.

Expedition after expedition set off into the rainforest in search of El Dorado's kingdom. One after another, they ended in disaster. Not a single European was swallowed whole by a man-eating snake, devoured by an alligator, or speared by a mythical headless Indian. The rainforest defeated them in a much slower, more agonizing way: It starved them to death.

Francisco Pizarro's brother Gonzalo led one of the first expeditions, in 1541. He left with 220 soldiers, 200 armored horses, 2,000 war hounds, and more than 2,000 pigs for food. Some 4,000 Indian slaves carried their supplies. Pizarro tortured indigenous villagers along the way, demanding that they tell him where the riches lay. When he wasn't satisfied with the answers, he had his captives burned to death or thrown to the dogs. Within a few months, nearly all the Indian slaves had fled into the jungle or died of smallpox.

By the end of the year, the Spaniards were starving. They heard animals everywhere but couldn't get close enough to take a shot. From time to time, they killed a small lizard or a snake and devoured it. Otherwise, they ate palm stalks and fruit pits that fell from the trees. When they had killed all their dogs and horses for food, they boiled the leather from boots and belts into a thin broth and drank it.

Finally, 80 emaciated men limped back to Quito. "They were so pale and disfigured that they were scarcely recognizable," reported a Spanish official.

A German expedition a couple of years earlier fared even worse. They resorted to cannibalism after 240 men died of disease and starvation. "Some, contrary to nature, ate human meat," reported an expedition member. "One Christian was found cooking a quarter of a child together with some greens."

Lope de Aguirre, the conquistador whose story Werner Herzog was filming when he tried to fly out of Lima on Christmas Eve, led yet another ill-fated expedition in search of El Dorado. In the heart of the rainforest, Aguirre rebelled against the Spanish king. He then murdered his own daughter before he was assassinated by his men. While still in the jungle, he wrote the king to tell him there were no riches hiding in the Amazon. "The reports are false," he said. "There is nothing on that river but despair."

To outsiders peering into the thick, dark forest, the Amazon became known as the "green hell."

That is not the way millions of rainforest natives would have described their home. Europeans often dismissed the indigenous people of the Amazon as "savages" or "barbarians." But the "savages" had one advantage over the "civilized" intruders: They knew how to survive in the jungle.

The conquistador Lope de Aguirre, as played by Klaus Kinski in Herzog's film *Aguirre, the Wrath of God.*

When the Europeans first arrived, the people of the Amazon had no access to metal, horses, or guns. There were no kingdoms rich enough to coat their kings in gold. But most communities supported themselves comfortably. Asháninka farmers in Peru cultivated manioc, a hardy root that doesn't need rich soil to grow. Throughout the rainforest, hunters wielded 10-foot-long blowguns with deadly accuracy, taking out birds and monkeys high in the treetops with poison darts. Fishermen learned to use a natural poison, scattering it in the water and scooping up fish when they surfaced to gasp for air. Riverside villages of the Omagua people in Brazil raised turtles for food and let nothing go to waste. Oil from the turtle eggs provided fuel for lamps. Turtle shells became bowls, and the jawbones became hatchets.

European explorers often marveled at how well the Indians lived off the land, but rarely did they learn to do it themselves. Instead, they tried to live off the Indians.

Francisco de Orellana, the Spaniard whose supposed encounter with women warriors gave the Amazon its name, traveled the entire river from west to east in the 1540s. He and his men attempted to hunt birds with crossbows and catch fish with lines and hooks. Usually, they came up empty-handed.

Orellana taught himself enough of the native languages to ask for food at villages along the way. Some Indians were kind—or scared—enough to hand over supplies. The Spaniards stocked up on "meats, partridges, turkeys, and fish of many sorts," recorded Gaspar de Carvajal, who kept a diary during the expedition. When negotiation didn't work, Orellana fought his way to the food supplies. Usually, the Indians were no match for the Spaniards' guns and crossbows.

Eventually, more and more Europeans came to the Amazon to settle—and they still relied on Indian labor to survive. On the rivers, indigenous men were enslaved to paddle white passengers from place to place. In the forest, Indian porters literally carried Spaniards on their backs. They wore harnesses with stirrups dangling below their waists for the lazy travelers' feet.

In the 1600s, a Portuguese priest named António Vieira pointed out just how helpless a European became in the rainforest. "For a man . . . to eat meat he needs a hunter; to eat fish a fisherman; to wear clean clothes a washerwoman; and to go to mass or anywhere else a canoe and paddlers . . . All the labor of the settlers is done by the native Indians."

Even the naturalists, who spent years studying the plants and animals of the Amazon, never understood the jungle as well as the men who paddled their boats. Richard Spruce, the Englishman who marveled at the size of the rainforest, once overheard a native man talking about him behind his back. "This man knows nothing," the Indian scoffed. "I doubt he can even shoot a bird with an arrow."

———◆———

By the time Juliane Koepcke was growing up in Peru, big cities had sprung up around the rainforest. The Incan capitals that Pizarro plundered had become tourist attractions. Roads were

A French book from the 19th century showed "the method of carrying travelers" in Colombia, on the northwest edge of the rainforest.

starting to open new areas of the forest to jeeps and trucks. Bulldozers hauled out trees to feed the timber industry. Planes scanned the forest with radar, looking for minerals to mine.

But even then, the Amazon was one of the most remote places on Earth. Vast areas had a population density less than two people per square mile. You could find more signs of human life than that in parts of the Sahara Desert.

A traveler dropped into the heart of the rainforest could walk for miles in any direction without meeting another human being. Trees? There were billions of them—some taller than a 20-story building. Animals? More than you could count—at least one-tenth of all the planet's species. Water? Gallons upon gallons—one-fifth of all the world's river water was in the Amazon River alone.

People, however, were few and far between. Hidden in the depths of the forest were more than 100 indigenous groups that had never been in contact with the outside world— people who had never seen a television, a phone, or a car.

And when outsiders strayed too far into the jungle, the results could still be disastrous. In 1970, an American journalist named Bob Nichols headed into Peru's Madre de Dios region with two French adventurers and six Mashco-Piro Indian guides. Like the Spanish conquistadors, they were hunting for a lost city—a legendary Incan hideaway called Paititi. The guides turned around when the expedition went too far for comfort.

Nichols and the two Frenchmen pressed on and were never heard from again.

People were still searching for them late in 1971, when LANSA Flight 508 disappeared into a storm over the largest rainforest in the world.

The rainforest of southeastern Peru as it looked two months before LANSA Flight 508 vanished.

CHAPTER 2

ALONE

Juliane Koepcke woke on Christmas Day 1971, curled in a ball on the rainforest floor under a row of airplane seats. She'd been dreaming—two dreams, braiding together in her mind. In one, she flew, soaring along a wall close to the ground. In the other, she was filthy with mud, dying to get up and wash herself off. Then she was flying again, barely avoiding the wall, with a roar so loud in her ears it was as though she herself had an engine. And then she lay in the mud again, desperate to get clean but unable to move.

It was like this for minutes or hours, back and forth between the two dreams until, still asleep, she said to herself, *Just get up and go wash yourself in the bathroom. It's simple.*

And suddenly, there she was, lying like a baby, face pressed toward the base of the seats with the seatbacks perched above her like a lean-to roof. She was covered in mud and drenched from head to foot. Vaguely, she remembered thunder and rain and crawling under the seats for shelter. All afternoon and night, she must have drifted from one dream to another, in and out of consciousness.

Now it was daytime. Far above the seatbacks, the treetops filtered sunlight into a dim, greenish glow. From above, she'd thought the trees looked like broccoli. Down here, they towered over her like skyscrapers. And gradually, all the pieces—the trees and the seats and the mud and the rain—began to make sense.

One minute, she had been sitting in the plane, her mother next to her and the sleeping man on the aisle. Lightning struck the plane, and in the next moment everyone had vanished. She was upside down in the seat, plummeting through the sky with the seat belt squeezing the breath out of her. When she dropped below the clouds, she saw the forest below.

Then she must have blacked out. She did not feel the impact when her seat hit the upper reaches of the trees, or the thrashing from the vines, or the final jolt when she struck the ground in a thick stew of mud and decaying leaves.

She had fallen from the plane in a storm, and somehow she had survived.

But had anyone else? Except for the row of seats, the plane seemed to be gone. The obese man in the aisle seat was gone. Her mother was gone.

Juliane crawled out from under the seats, the thought forming in her mind that she had to find her mother. She made it to her knees before everything went black and she crumpled to the ground.

A Brazil-nut tree towers over the forest floor in southeastern Peru.

When she managed to pull herself to a sitting position, she looked at her watch. It was ticking, so she knew it worked, but she couldn't bring the face of the watch into focus. Her glasses had vanished, and her eyes were in bad shape. The left eye had swollen shut, and the right one had narrowed to a slit barely big enough to see through. She squinted until the face of the watch came into focus: 9:00.

She tried again to stand. The earth spun, and she collapsed. Her head felt as though it were packed in cotton. For the moment she was helpless, and a desperate loneliness began to settle around her. Everyone was gone, and she had no idea where she was.

Finally, after a few more tries, she stood. As she began to move, her body came back to her. Her hand found its way to a lump just below her neck—a bone pressing against the skin as though it were trying to push through. Her collarbone had broken on the right side like a stick snapped not quite in two. On the lower part of her left leg, something sharp had torn a gruesome-looking gash in the flesh. The cut ran at least an inch and a half long and an inch deep. She found another puncture the size of a coin on the triceps of her right arm.

For some reason, the wounds weren't bleeding, and she felt no pain. She had just fallen more than half a mile from an airplane to the earth and nothing hurt.

But where was everyone else? If she had survived, she thought, others must have too. She called out for her mother.

The forest gave up no sign of human life. She dropped to her knees and crawled through the dirt and decaying leaves. Again and again, she yelled for her mother. Only the frogs responded, with a strange chorus of clicks and chirps.

Juliane felt abandoned and utterly alone. The world around her seemed familiar from her time at Panguana. And yet, the rainforest has a way of making humans feel like they don't belong. The canopy created by the treetops screens out 95 percent of the sun's light and shrouds the ground in perpetual twilight. There's life everywhere, but it rarely makes itself visible. Sitting on the forest floor, you hear leaves rustle and birds screech. High overhead, creatures move from tree to tree—sloths and howler monkeys, parrots and raptors. Leafcutter ants climb 100 feet to chew greenery, then transport it belowground, where it feeds fungus that transforms the leaves back into nutrients for the trees. Life cycles that have been established for thousands—even millions—of years play themselves out with no regard at all for human beings.

The naturalist Alfred Russell Wallace spent years collecting specimens in the Amazon in the mid-1800s, and he never quite got used to it. "There is a weird gloom and a solemn silence," he wrote, "which combine to produce a sense of the vast—the primeval—world of the infinite. It is a world in which man seems an intruder."

Juliane tested her legs again, ready to search for a sign of the world she had been torn from 24 hours before. She had boarded the plane in a pair of flimsy sandals, open at the heel. Only one of them had survived the fall. By instinct, she kept it on. In the rainforest, she had always worn tough rubber boots to protect against snakes; now, some protection seemed better than none.

Slowly, she began to walk in circles around the airplane seat. There was really no good reason to stay close to it, but she didn't stray. As far as she could see, the seat was the only sign of civilization besides herself.

Far above her, the canopy looked undisturbed. If the LANSA flight had crash-landed nearby, it would have cut a long scar through the treetops. Instead, a tangled, unbroken web of vines, known as lianas, hung from the branches and trunks.

In the rainforest, lianas are champions in the vicious competition for survival. They start life as a sprout on the light-starved floor of the forest and climb toward the sun by any means necessary. They wrap themselves around tree trunks, even other vines, until they reach the canopy. The strongest lianas grow as thick as a human thigh. When they reach the light, they can sprout leaves the size of bedsheets and cut off the sun's rays, starving the trees that gave them life in the first place.

Juliane probably had these hardened survivors to thank for her own survival. Unless some unseen force had slowed her on the way down, she had plummeted into the treetops at 120 miles an hour. The lianas, along with the tree branches in the canopy, must have acted like a rough-hewn net. They pummeled

Gnarled lianas battle for space in the rainforest near Iquitos, Peru.

her on the way down. Most likely they were responsible for her collarbone, the swollen eyes, the gash in her calf, and whatever was making it hard to stand without the entire world spinning around her. But once they had bruised her, they had, unthinkably, delivered her to the ground alive.

"Hello!" she cried out. "Is anyone there?"

Again and again, she yelled into the vines and the trees. Only the frogs replied.

She broadened her circles from the row of seats, combing the area for signs of the plane. On the sodden ground she found a bag of hard candies and a panettone, the Italian Christmas cake that Peruvians had adopted for the holidays. She tore off a piece of the cake and tried to eat it, but it was soggy and covered in mud. It tasted disgusting. She kept the candies and left the panettone where it lay.

Then came another sign from the world beyond the trees. A plane engine whined above the canopy, and then another. People were searching for her . . . for all of them . . . for anyone who might be left. But whatever comfort the sound brought vanished as soon as Juliane looked overhead. The dense canopy that kept light from reaching the rainforest floor also kept the sight of anything on the ground from reaching the sky. From above, there was only dense forest. No pilot, no matter how carefully he looked, would ever be able to see her.

Juliane still felt like her brain was packed in cotton. She had suffered a concussion during her plunge to the ground. She was also in a state of shock that could easily have paralyzed her. In 1945, when the United States dropped atomic bombs on Hiroshima and Nagasaki at the end of World War II, the Japanese noticed that many of the survivors seemed unable to make decisions. They called the reaction *burabura*, or "do-nothing sickness." It's a state that often affects people in times of extreme stress.

Alone in the rainforest after plummeting from the sky, Juliane could easily have turned her airplane seat over, sat down, and waited for someone to save her. Instead, she decided that if she did nothing, she was dead. Somehow, she had to get herself to a clearing so the pilots could find her. She might even have to find her way back to civilization by herself.

Just how she was going to make that happen remained unclear.

It is notoriously hard to navigate in the rainforest without a compass. Hikers in deciduous forests can tell direction by the path of the sun. But the rainforest canopy makes it hard to pinpoint the sun in the sky. Indigenous travelers learned to mark their path by breaking branches or hacking marks into trees with a machete. But that practice only led you back to your starting point. Juliane needed to get away from her patch of the Amazon, with its battered airplane seats and its mud-soaked Christmas cake. And even a compass would have done her little good. Since she had no idea where she was starting from, she had no idea which way to go.

The forest felt familiar to her, and that was a good sign. The species of trees, the bird calls, the frog noises—she knew them all from the long walks she had taken with her parents at Panguana, learning to identify birds and plants. It could be that she wasn't far from home. But even if that were true, any direction she chose might take her deeper into untraveled land.

It was a terrible feeling. Get lost in the city or the suburbs, and you may not know which way to go, but you have routes to follow—roads or paths that will lead you somewhere. When outsiders get lost in the forest, they have nothing familiar to

Juliane as a young girl, in the forest with her mother.

guide them. The American explorer Gene Savoy went hunting for a lost Incan city in the Peruvian wilderness in 1964. His crew spent one day hacking their way through the jungle with machetes, only to come full circle to a trail they had cut earlier. "Strange how the shallow little footpath of the day before gives the men a sense of assurance," he wrote later. "Even I feel it. It is our mark upon the jungle, a meandering ribbon we had claimed from the unknown. It is our link with the outside world. A trail is everything in the jungle. Without it a man is unsure of himself, on unfamiliar ground."

Juliane had no trail. But she had something almost as good—a childhood spent in the rainforest.

When she had been living at Panguana, a young student had stumbled into the research station, weak, exhausted, and hungry. He had left weeks earlier for the nearby Sira Mountains with a group of scientists from California. When one of the men accidentally shot himself, the student set out to get help. He lost the trail and wandered helplessly in the forest—until he found water and followed it downstream. A stream led him to a river, which eventually led him to Panguana.

It was advice she had heard again and again from her father. When she set out on her own for walks around Panguana, he had told her in his gruff, protective way that if she got lost she had to follow the water. Even the smallest of creeks would lead eventually to a river. And all rivers led eventually to people.

As Juliane made her way around the row of seats, still dazed, the planes above her moved on, leaving only the sounds of the forest behind. Under the rustling and the chirping and the buzzing, another sound emerged—a quiet trickling that must have been there all along. Now she recognized it as her lifeline: moving water.

CHAPTER 3

FOLLOW THE WATER

A t 1 p.m. on Christmas Eve day, around the time Juliane Koepcke plunged from the sky, Floyd Lyon watched a roiling mass of cumulus clouds close in from the south. He sat at the flight coordinator's office of the Summer Institute for Linguistics in Yarinacocha, a missionary community just outside of Pucallpa. The "linguistics," as people called them, translated the Christian Bible into indigenous languages. They also offered education, medical care, and other services to indigenous villages in the area.

Lyon and his fellow missionary pilots often flew small double-engine planes into the rainforest to deliver supplies or hold classes. He knew it wasn't a good idea to be aloft in a storm like the one he saw approaching. And that's exactly where his son Nathan was—the same Nathan Lyon who had shared a joke with Juliane just a couple of hours before at the Lima airport.

By 1:15, the storm hit Yarinacocha with startling fury. Flight 508 had missed its landing time by a half hour, and Lyon was on the two-way radio listening to the air traffic controllers. He had heard the plane call in over Oyon, in the mountains. After that, he heard other ground stations trying to reach the pilot on the radio. "No contact," they reported, again and again.

At 1:45, Lyon called the institute's main office. Besides Nathan and his friend David Ericson, the plane had been carrying three other members of the community. Their friends and relatives on the ground were getting anxious. Over the roar of thunder, Lyon told them the plane appeared to be lost. "It doesn't look good," he said.

The next morning, the news hadn't improved. All the newspapers in Peru announced the plane's disappearance. LANSA PLANE LOST; 92 ABOARD: TRAGEDY ON CHRISTMAS EVE? read the headline in *La Nueva Crónica*.

By 6 a.m., search parties were headed into the jungle with medical supplies and food. Six planes had taken off to comb the area between Huanuco and Pucallpa. Three of those planes belonged to the linguistics. Floyd Lyon stayed at the base, monitoring the radio and hoping for news of his son.

That morning, an air force colonel arrived in Pucallpa to direct what would soon become the largest search and rescue operation in Peruvian history. He found the city nearly empty and the airport packed with people. Fifty-five of the plane's passengers had been bound for Pucallpa. Their family members and friends now crowded the LANSA counter at the tiny airport, demanding to know what had happened.

Friends and family of the LANSA passengers gather at the Lima airport, hoping for news of the flight.

Rumors had already started to fly: The Electra had landed in Iquitos, in Huanuco; a villager had seen it crash into a hillside 20 miles south of Pucallpa; a radio station reported that the plane had been found in the jungle.

A spokesman from the Ministry of Aviation showed up long enough to declare, "any rumor that has circulated is false."

Tempers rose when the airline couldn't offer anything more satisfying than that. A reporter overheard one of the family members yelling at a LANSA spokesman: "You can't even carry a brick, and yet you dare to transport people!"

By 6 p.m., darkness was beginning to fall, and the search planes were called in. None of the pilots had seen a thing. The crowd at the airport thinned. Some people settled in for an overnight vigil. Others went home to their Christmas decorations. Still others answered a call to go to the hospital and donate blood, hoping it would soon be needed.

———◆———

For hours in the afternoon, the hum of the planes taunted Juliane. They came and went overhead, invisible and ineffective. If she could not see them, they certainly couldn't see her. She still had trouble thinking clearly, but one thought was sharp enough to pierce the fog: She had to find a clearing. The trees had always been a haven to her. Now, if she didn't move, they would become her coffin.

It hadn't taken her long to find the source of the trickling sound. A spring burbled from the ground not far from the airplane seats. From it a small rivulet of water ran away downhill. The flow wasn't big enough to call a stream, and yet the sight filled her with hope.

Juliane knelt and drank her fill. She cupped her hands, filled them with spring water, and washed away as much of the dirt as she could. Then she set off to follow the water, with only the bag of hard candies for supplies.

In all her years in the rainforest, Juliane had never been more ill equipped. She had one sandal between her and the forest floor. Only a thin minidress with a broken zipper in the back protected her from the swarms of mosquitoes and black flies. Without her glasses, everything more than a few yards away faded to a blur.

Following the rivulet was no easy task. She had to climb over dead logs and find her way around knots of tangled underbrush. After a time, the trickle widened into a real streambed, about a foot and a half across. The water rarely filled the bed all the way, but the stream seemed to be getting bigger.

At around 6 p.m., the half-light on the forest floor faded to true darkness. The hum of the planes had vanished, and Juliane found a place by the side of the streambed to rest for the night. She dug a candy out of the bag and savored the sweet, fruity taste. Then she lay back to sleep.

———◉———

If the Amazon makes humans feel like intruders during the day, it can scare them out of their wits at night. When the sun goes down, the rainforest wakes up. Out of the dark comes a bewildering variety of sounds. Over the shrill whistle of the cicadas and the locusts, wood rails cackle and toucans screech. Mosquitoes whine in one ear, then the other. Frogs make noises that no outsider would ever attribute to a small, slimy amphibian. "A distant railway-train approaching, and a black-smith hammering on his anvil, are what they exactly resemble," said Alfred Russell Wallace. In the middle of it all comes the deep roar of the howler monkey, which sounds like a prehistoric, man-eating dinosaur hidden in the trees.

A twenty-two-year-old Israeli backpacker named Yossi Ghinsberg spent three weeks lost in the rainforest in 1981, and he barely survived the nights. He and two others followed a

The call of the howler monkey can be heard up to 2 miles away.

guide deep into the forest in Bolivia to pan for gold. Low on food and hopelessly lost, the expedition split up. Ghinsberg and a friend climbed aboard a makeshift raft and tried to ride a dangerous river back to civilization. When the friend went overboard and the raft shattered in churning rapids, Ghinsberg was left alone in the jungle.

As he wandered by himself, searching for his friend, he dreaded the end of the day. In the dark, the noises drove him wild with panic. Every screech made him imagine a jaguar ripping a monkey limb from limb. He slept with a lighter and an aerosol can of bug spray next to him, ready to torch a salivating predator. "I had never been so terrified," he wrote. "I kept hearing sounds all around me, and my heart was pounding frantically. *God, just don't let a wild animal devour me.*"

———◆———

Four hundred miles west of Yossi Ghinsberg's "green hell," Juliane slept like a baby. Her concussion was partly responsible, but she also knew where the real dangers of the rainforest lay. For two years she had gone to sleep at Panguana with the sounds of the jungle in her ears. The frogs sounded like frogs to her, the birds like birds, the howler monkeys like howler monkeys. She knew that jaguars did not generally hunt people. If death came in the forest, it would probably not be at the jaws of a hungry predator.

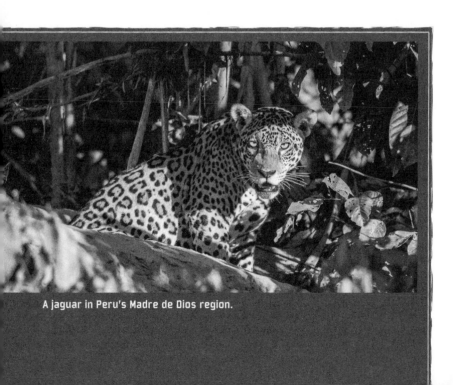
A jaguar in Peru's Madre de Dios region.

Juliane woke the day after Christmas, her sleep undisturbed by beasts. Somewhere overhead, the sun had risen, but she couldn't see it. Like yesterday, the treetops hid the sky. And once again, they would hide her from the pilots combing the forest for signs of the plane. She still felt lazy and slow from the concussion, but she knew that if she wanted to live she had to move.

As she worked her way down the streambed, she made painfully slow progress. She shoved aside underbrush and clambered over logs. When she wasn't sure what lay in front of her—ants or spiders or snakes—she led with her sandaled foot.

She hadn't gone far when she came eye to eye with the kind of creature that had given the rainforest its reputation as a place of unspeakable horrors. Perched on a branch just across the stream was a spider the size of her hand. She knew it immediately as a Goliath birdeater, a species of tarantula that can weigh more than a small parrot.

Like many rainforest creatures, the Goliath doesn't quite live up to its fearsome reputation: It rarely attacks birds. But with fangs that can grow up to an inch and a half long, it's been known to devour toads, frogs, small rodents, and snakes. The Goliath doesn't pack enough venom to be deadly to humans, but it can cause tremendous pain.

The spider eyed Juliane for a few seconds, and she stared back at it. Then they both moved on, the Goliath making audible, clicking footsteps as it scuttled away.

The Goliath birdeater is the largest spider on Earth.

As the hours wore on, Juliane clung to the stream, step after step. Her father's words rang in her ear: *Follow the water.* Aside from that, the concussion clouded her thoughts. Only a vague set of assumptions kept her moving. She assumed that if she had survived, there must be others alive too. She assumed she would make it back to safety somehow. The waterway kept getting wider; it had to lead to a river, to a clearing, maybe to a village or a logging outpost. She heard the planes from time to time and yelled into the treetops.

———◆———

Another night passed, and the third day began like the day before—the dim light of daytime in the forest, the obstacle course by the side of the stream. In the morning, mosquitoes and black flies descended on her. They attacked every inch of exposed skin, hungry for blood. The swarms were so thick it did no good to fight them off.

Then again, swarming insects had been constant companions during the long hours she had spent doing research with her mother. To Maria, endurance in the forest had been a point of pride. Once, they'd been watching a nest of sun bitterns together. When Juliane started to squirm under an onslaught of mosquitoes, her mother told her not to move. "If you want to be a biologist," she said, "you must learn to sacrifice."

By midday, the temperature had climbed into the 90s, and the heat drove the insects away. As Juliane picked her way carefully through the streambed, a large shape appeared in the distance, blocking her path. Gradually, it came into focus—something foreign to the jungle but familiar to her.

It was a bullet-shaped hunk of metal with a propeller attached, maybe 20 feet long and at least as tall as a person. When she'd last seen it, she had been staring out the window of the LANSA plane into the storm. One side of the engine had been blackened by fire. The rest of the wing was nowhere to be seen.

Three days ago, the engine had helped lift 92 people into the sky. Now it lay earthbound, covered in mud in a remote rainforest stream. Juliane stared at the dead hunk of metal for a while. The charring must have come from the lightning strike she had seen outside her window in the heart of the storm.

She regarded the engine with a vague amazement, feeling strangely removed from what it meant. The sight did not bring back her mother's voice, declaring that the end had come. It did not make her visualize an entire airplane breaking into pieces in midair. She made her way around the engine as though it were another fallen tree and followed the stream.

———◆———

The next day, December 28, Juliane's watch stopped. She had been walking for three days, and the engine was still the only sign she'd seen that the plane or its passengers had ever existed.

Now, as she pushed her way through vines and clambered over logs, she heard a noise that sent a chill through her veins. It was the sound of wings beating the air—not the flutter of small parakeets or hummingbirds, but the distinct *whomping* of very large wings.

She knew what kind of bird it was before she saw it: the *cóndor de la selva*, or king vulture. She also knew that the king vulture, with its 6-foot wingspan, rarely bothers with dead tree squirrels or small snakes. It only comes out to feast when large amounts of food are available.

Juliane pressed ahead through a gathering cloud of dread. Around the next bend in the stream, several vultures sat high

The king vulture has a beak strong enough to tear through the toughest carcasses.

in the trees, waiting. Below them lay a row of airplane seats, just like the one that carried Juliane from the plane to the forest floor—only this row of seats had landed upside down with the seatbacks buried three feet deep in mud. Sticking up from the seats were three sets of human legs.

CHAPTER 4

NO SHORTCUTS

Juliane stared in terror at the three corpses, strapped to their seats and half buried in the mud. Only once before had she seen a dead body, at an open-casket reception for a child who had died. She was six at the time, and she had been fascinated.

Now, 11 years later, the sight left her horrified. Ever since she'd woken up under the airplane seats, she had been wandering in a daze. The full impact of the disaster hadn't reached her. Maybe it was the concussion. Maybe it was simply the brain's way of protecting her from trauma while she battled for her life. But here was evidence she could not ignore: Three people who could have been sitting just in front of her or across the aisle on the plane now lay dead on the forest floor.

Then another thought filled her with terror: *What if one of the bodies belonged to her mother?*

She made herself step toward the seats. Thankfully, the king vultures hadn't started their work yet, but the sharp buzzing of flies filled the air. The voracious little creatures wasted no time laying their eggs in body cavities and open wounds. In the rainforest, the dead are recycled instantly into nutrients by insects, birds, and bacteria. Animal corpses are usually reduced to bones in a matter of days.

Juliane crept closer, revolted by the sight of the legs, still belted to the seats. Judging from the pants and the shoes, two of the bodies had been men. She poked tentatively at the feet of the third body with a stick and revealed a set of painted toenails. Her mother, she thought with relief, never painted her nails.

Then she realized that her mother had been belted into the seat right next to her. *How could she have been so dense?* Painted toenails or no, this woman could not have been her mother from the start.

———◆———

By Monday, the day before Juliane found the bodies, the air search had expanded to a dozen planes. Pucallpa was a hive of activity. Planes landed, refueled, and took off again. Vans carried search patrols out of the city southward toward the town of Puerto Inca. Local telephone lines were clogged with calls from Iquitos and Lima. People camped out at the airport, pressing anyone who looked official for news.

Bob Weninger, a missionary pilot from Wisconsin who had been flying in South America for five years, landed in Pucallpa on Monday to join the search. He had to fight off parents, sisters, and uncles of lost passengers who were desperate to fly

with him. Everyone, it seemed, was certain that if they could just get close to the crash site they would discover their loved ones miraculously alive and well.

Weninger wasn't ready to call it false hope. In 1967, he remembered, a Brazilian military plane had run out of fuel over the rainforest and ditched in a swamp. Ten days went by before a search plane spotted vultures circling above the trees. Rescuers found 5 of the plane's 25 passengers injured and unable to walk but still alive.

That morning, a picture of two adorable kids appeared in *La Nueva Crónica*—a girl of about five or six with her arm around her little brother's shoulders. Their father was identified as José Guererro Rovalino, the accountant who had been to Lima on business and told his mother that he didn't want to fly

LANSA home. The caption below the kids read, *Will they be orphans now?*

———◆———

After four days of dry weather, the rain returned on Wednesday, the day after Juliane found the bodies. By midday it was pouring in the forest. The hum of the search plane engines had been a near constant presence during the daylight hours. Now the sound faded and disappeared altogether.

For Juliane, the effects of the concussion were fading, and she could think more clearly. But aside from a few handfuls of hard candy, she hadn't eaten since breakfast on the plane Friday morning. She didn't feel hungry exactly, but she knew she was getting weaker.

She trudged on, leading with her sandaled foot to put something between her skin and the forest floor. When the jungle closed off her path on the stream bank, she waded in the middle of the water. In places, the underbrush grew so thick she had to wander off track to find her way around and back to the stream. She had nothing but her hands to fight off a tangle of growth so dense that it has defeated even the most experienced explorers.

The Scottish scientist James Murray had been almost to the South Pole and back before he ventured into the Amazon in 1911. He fell behind the rest of his expedition, and by the end of the trip, his feet were swollen and raw. Open sores ravaged his body, leaking pus and infested with maggots. He insisted he was only alive because he'd been able to hack his way through the runaway growth that threatened to swallow him at every turn. "Without a machete," he said, "it means death to be lost in such forest."

Juliane had no machete, no sleeping bag, no tent, and nothing but a dwindling supply of hard candies for food. Most of all, she was beginning to feel as though she had no time. At some point, the authorities in Lima or Pucallpa would decide that no one had survived the crash. They would call off the search or scale it way back. If she didn't find a clearing quickly, there would be no planes to spot her. She had no idea how much ground she was covering, but she couldn't have been moving fast.

Like most Amazon waterways, Juliane's stream meandered in loops like a slithering snake. It's not unusual for a rainforest stream or river to travel four or five times longer than a straight line drawn through the center of its path. Juliane could hear her father's voice: *Stick to the water; don't take shortcuts.* But if she could just cut straight through the forest from bend to bend, she would save hours, if not days, in the end.

During five centuries of ill-fated expeditions in the Amazon, it was a temptation that had proved hard to resist.

———◆———

On October 1, 1769, just over 200 years before Juliane fell into the rainforest, a strange parade of travelers left the town of Riobamba, in the mountains of Spanish Peru. Thirty-one

Most rivers in the Amazon follow a long, winding path through the forest.

Puruhá Indian porters labored down cliffside trails toward the lowland forest. They dragged with them trunks and packs loaded with silver bowls, fine china, linens, and a lady's wardrobe, including lace underwear, shawls, and shoes with gleaming gold buckles. They also carried the lady herself.

In a sedan chair supported on the shoulders of several Puruhás sat Isabel Godin, descendant of Spanish conquistadors. She wore an outfit about as appropriate for a rainforest expedition as Juliane's minidress—a long, billowing dress and dainty cotton shoes. Her silver bracelets and gold necklaces jingled as she bounced along.

She may have overdressed for the occasion, but Isabel could hardly be considered soft. At the time, women of her class in

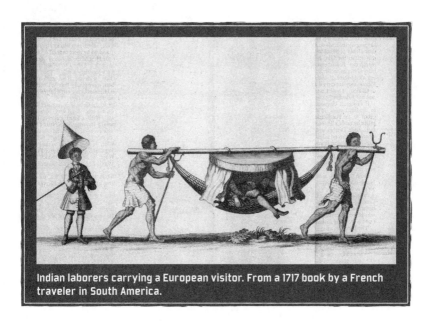

Indian laborers carrying a European visitor. From a 1717 book by a French traveler in South America.

the Spanish colonies rarely even visited neighbors without a maid or husband escorting them. Isabel was setting out to cross 2,000 miles of largely uncharted rainforest.

Her aim was to reunite with her husband, a French engineer who had been shut out of Peru by Spanish authorities. In addition to the porters, Isabel had her two brothers, a black slave named Joachim, and several other companions along for the ride.

It didn't take long for the expedition to fall apart. After a week on muddy, mountainous trails, Isabel was carried like a queen into a village of smoldering huts. The Puruhá porters knew only too well what they were looking at. The town had been ravaged by smallpox and burned to the ground in an

Isabel Godin on her disastrous trek through the Peruvian Amazon.

attempt to kill the disease. In the 270 years since white explorers first arrived in the Americas, European germs—with smallpox at the head of the list—had wiped out millions of Indians. The Puruhás had no desire to become the next victims. All 31 of them fled into the rainforest.

Isabel and her companions left the sedan chair to rot and traveled on by canoe down the Bobonaza River. When the overstuffed boat hit a log and tipped, the party found themselves stranded on a riverbank. Joachim and two others paddled off again with a much lighter load. They promised to come back with a rescue party.

Isabel and the rest waited more than three weeks for Joachim to return. Finally, starving and ravaged by mosquitoes, they decided to move. Isabel traded her ragged silks for a pair of pants from one of her brothers, and the desperate crew headed downriver.

That's when they ran into the dilemma that has plagued many a traveler in the Amazon. Like Juliane's stream, the Bobonaza wandered in a broad, endless "S" pattern. A dense tangle of underbrush and lianas clogged the banks. Frustrated by their creeping pace, Isabel and her brothers made a fateful decision. "By keeping along the river's side," Isabel's husband later reported, "they found its sinuosities greatly length-ened their way, to avoid which inconvenience they penetrated the wood."

For Isabel's companions, it would be the final mistake. Hours after they left the riverbank, the travelers were hopelessly lost.

They dragged themselves through the jungle, hoping to stumble onto the Bobonaza again. After three or four weeks, they lay on the rainforest floor, unable to move. Isabel watched her two brothers die slowly of starvation and dehydration. In their final days, they were little more than food for swarms of hungry insects.

Horrified by the decaying corpses, Isabel found the strength to move on. She staggered through the forest, found the riverbank, and collapsed at the feet of a very surprised Indian couple, who brought her to the next town downriver. There she learned that Joachim had returned to their original camp on the riverbank more than a month earlier. Help had come just a week after they decided to shortcut the river bends and "penetrate the wood."

With her father's advice in her ear, Juliane stuck to the stream. She plodded for hours through the dim light, the rain coming more often now. It was Wednesday, maybe Thursday, when she heard a scratchy, rhythmic call in the distance. Someone who didn't know the forest might easily have thought a metalworker had set up shop in the trees with a handsaw. But the same noise had often filled the air around Panguana, and Juliane knew exactly what made it—a chicken-sized bird called a hoatzin. Hoatzins have scraggly orange crests that make them look like goths with spiked and dyed mohawks. Their chicks are born with claws on the "elbows" of their wings, like their distant ancestor, the archaeopteryx.

Hoatzins perched near a river in southeastern Peru.

Juliane knew all of this because her mother had studied the birds. And thanks to her mother, she knew another thing about hoatzins: They nest only on the banks of relatively large rivers.

The wheezy call of the birds pulled Juliane forward with a new urgency. Before long, she could see her little stream emptying into a broad channel, rich with churning brown water and measuring at least 30 feet across. Nearly a week after Flight 508 ejected her high over the rainforest, she had found her way to a real river.

The forest made her pay to get there. A thick maze of dead logs and underbrush blocked the intersection of the stream and the river. She fought painfully through a patch of razor-sharp cana brava reeds that towered over her head. It took hours to get around the underbrush, but finally Juliane found herself standing on the banks of a broad waterway. Above her was a sight she had not seen in days: a clear, uninterrupted swath of sky.

After nearly a week imprisoned in the jungle she had found two pathways out—the river and the sky. They were two links, however tentative, to the world she had left behind.

Plane engines hummed in the distance for a while, well out of sight. *Why weren't they coming closer?* When she'd been hidden, they had sounded near enough to touch. Now that the sky lay open above her, they were nowhere to be seen. Finally, a plane appeared above the gap in the trees. She yelled and waved her arms in the air, but the pilot veered off and disappeared over the canopy.

As the day wore on, Juliane's spirits fell. The sound of the engines disappeared altogether. The sky looked angry, and rain fell hard and often. The river that had inspired so much hope a few hours ago now looked like a wild, untraveled piece of the jungle. Driftwood and giant logs floated in the current; no boat would dare try to navigate this river.

And where were the planes? They had given up the search; she was sure of it. They had probably found the rest of the survivors and airlifted them to safety. No one had any idea she was still wandering the forest floor, hopelessly lost and alone.

CHAPTER 5

THE RIVER

O n Wednesday, December 29, dozens of Pucallpa residents spent the day hacking through the jungle with machetes, looking for signs that the 4-engine plane had eased itself through the trees on Christmas Eve and made a landing on the forest floor. Adolfo Saldana was one of the searchers. His son Roger had been coming home from college for Christmas on Flight 508. Saldana had joined a civilian patrol and headed into the forest, hoping to find his son alive.

The patrols moved at a painfully slow pace. Rain had flooded parts of the forest and turned others to thick, slimy mud. The families had pooled their resources to buy supplies for the patrols, but transporting them into the forest wasn't easy. They had asked Commander Teddy del Carpio, head of search operations, for a helicopter. Del Carpio refused, insisting the helicopter would be used only to evacuate survivors—if they were lucky enough to find any.

On Wednesday night, done with his work until the next day, Saldana got on the road to drive home to Pucallpa. Like

A search patrol hacks its way through the forest near the Pachitea River the day before Saldana's death.

most routes through the rainforest, the "highway" was unpaved and riddled with ruts. Just after dark, he tried to negotiate a curve and skidded in the mud. His car rolled onto its hood and smashed into a tree. Adolfo Saldana was killed on impact.

Under grim skies and the shadow of Saldana's death, the search efforts stalled. On Thursday, three planes took off from Pucallpa. They were enveloped by storm clouds and had to turn around. Friday—New Year's Eve—was not much better. Commander del Carpio grew worried he would lose more family members to the weather. As people gathered for Saldana's funeral in Pucallpa, del Carpio set up guards to stop any new civilian patrols from venturing into the jungle.

When the clouds broke for an hour or two, a few planes tried to take off. Bob Weninger flew whenever he could get aloft. Usually, a new storm forced him back to base before he could cover much ground. Even when skies were clear, all the pilots could see was an endless carpet of green. A flier from the missionary base at Yarinacocha told a reporter: "It's like looking for a needle in a haystack."

———◆———

Juliane had no idea that Adolfo Saldana had died. She didn't know that police were trying to prevent people from searching for her. But she definitely felt as small and insignificant as a needle in a haystack. She had discovered a river—and it had not led her to people. She had found an opening to the sky—but the planes that had patrolled it for days seemed to have vanished.

Emotions that had started to surface when she found the bodies now broke through. Staring at the empty sliver of sky, she grew furious. *How could they stop searching less than a week after the crash? If they had found other survivors, why wouldn't they keep looking for her?*

The anger turned quickly to despair. She had fooled herself into thinking that water would save her—that if she found a river she would find people. Well, she had done it, and look where her efforts had gotten her. No canoe had ever tried to navigate this dismal stretch of water; it looked like a grave-yard for half the trees in the rainforest. And nothing about the landscape suggested that it had ever played host to a human being. There were no broken branches to mark a once-traveled path, no pile of palm fronds from a collapsed shelter.

She'd been fighting the rainforest with her bare hands in nothing but a minidress and one sandal and she was no closer to civilization than she had been at the start. Open wounds on her calf and her arm were in danger of becoming infected. She'd had no real food for nearly a week. She was little more than a walking meal for the mosquitoes and black flies. Why shouldn't she just find a tree to lean against and wait for what-ever came?

As it had so often since Saturday, her father's voice came back to her. It had become a mantra, a motto, something

Hans and Maria Koepcke, surrounded by collections from their research.

she didn't have to summon: *Follow the river; rivers lead to people.*

Juliane knew that Hans Koepcke was not one to sit on a riverbank and wait. As a young man, he had been so determined to get to Peru that he had walked most of the way from Germany. Had there not been an ocean in his path, he probably would have made the entire journey on foot.

World War II had just ended, and Hans wanted to make a name for himself as a biologist. He knew the best place to do it was in the rainforest. When the natural history museum in Lima offered him a job, he set out on foot. He crawled under the border fence into Austria and hitchhiked to Italy. He crossed a minefield to France and climbed a mountain range to

Spain. From there he hid himself in a pile of salt on a freighter and made it to the coast of Brazil. He was out of money but ecstatic that he had finally made it to the rainforest. So to get to Peru, he walked more than 2,000 miles across the continent, studying the forest along the way.

Hans Koepcke had left Germany in 1948; he arrived in Lima in 1950. In contrast to so many of the naturalists and explorers who had come before him, he mastered the jungle. "When we have really resolved to achieve something, we succeed," he liked to say. "We only have to want it."

Juliane did not feel especially close to her father. He was the kind of man you respected, not the kind of man you adored. But he had a presence that was hard to ignore. After 17 years listening to his lessons and living up to his expectations, Juliane too had become the kind of person who could not sit on a riverbank and wait. With the skies still threatening, she picked herself up and began to follow the water.

———◆———

For centuries, rivers have been the arteries of human civilization in the Amazon. Indigenous craftsmen carved 40-foot dugout canoes from individual tree trunks. They navigated churning rapids with ease. They feasted on bass, catfish, eel, and turtles pulled with great skill from river waters.

The white colonists who arrived in the 16th century needed the rivers to transport goods and people. Like Isabel Godin, they lost their way as soon as they strayed into the forest. But they had no idea how to negotiate the whirlpools and unpredictable

For its weight, the piranha has a bite stronger than nearly any meat-eating creature on Earth.

currents of rainforest rivers, so they enslaved Indian boatmen to navigate for them. And the waters themselves were a mysterious place. Hidden beneath the surface were creatures that bit, shocked, and killed in ways that fired the imaginations of frightened travelers.

South American alligators, known as caimans, lay all day in the weeds of the riverbanks, disguised as logs. At night they slipped into the water to hunt. Their eyes, big as plums, gleamed in the moonlight. The naturalists Jorge Juan and Antonio de Ulloa insisted that once caimans got a taste of human flesh they would do anything to get more.

Piranha fish, with their jutting lower jaws and razor-like teeth, had a particularly bloodthirsty reputation. Former U.S. president Teddy Roosevelt, who traveled in the Amazon after leaving the White House, claimed he once saw a school of piranhas turn a cow into a skeleton in minutes. "They will rend and devour alive any wounded man or beast," he reported, "for blood in the water excites them to madness."

The *puraque*, or electric eel, attacked in an even more exotic way: It gave its victims a 650-volt shock. In 1799, the German naturalist Alexander Humboldt sent a few horses into an eel-infested bog to observe their reaction. Their manes stood on end and they scrambled for dry land. Two of the unfortunate creatures gave up their lives to science, drowning in the bog.

But it was the needle-shaped candiru that inspired the worst nightmares of all. This tiny parasitic catfish swam into body cavities, opened spines along its body, and latched on to feast on the blood of its host. The candiru normally fed in the gills of other fish. But it was said to possess a skill that was of special interest to anyone who considered relieving himself in a river. Supposedly, the candiru could swim up a stream of urine and lodge itself in a human urethra.

———◆———

As Juliane made her way downstream, she knew the legendary reputations of the river creatures. She also knew the difference between real and imagined dangers. She tried to stick to the

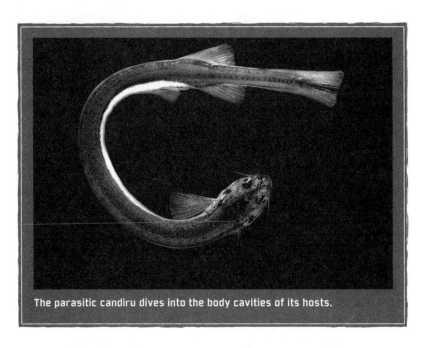

The parasitic candiru dives into the body cavities of its hosts.

banks. But without a machete, she didn't make much progress. The underbrush scraped at her arms and legs. Vines swiped at her head. The tangled growth pushed her into the shallows, where she picked her way across sharp and slippery rocks. She poked at the riverbed with a stick before each step, looking not for voracious piranhas or bloodsucking candirus, but for stingrays.

To people who know the rainforest, stingrays inspire more fear and caution than 16-foot caimans. They lie on the river's floor, camouflaged in mud. If a foot disturbs their rest, they lash out with a barbed tail sharp enough to slice through a rubber boot. Their poison won't kill a human unless it strikes a vital organ. But in Juliane's case, it wouldn't need to. In her weakened state, a wound from a 5-inch stingray spike could leave her unable to walk for days—and that would be enough.

In the shallows, Juliane stumbled along in a ritual pattern: stick first, then sandal, then bare foot. Slippery rocks and overhanging vines tormented her. She made slow and painful progress, and after a while she decided to slip into the middle of the river and drift with the current. Churning silt turned the water a murky brown. She could have been escorted by a river full of piranhas, and she wouldn't have known it.

More than once, as she swam in the murk, Juliane startled a caiman dozing on the bank. What happened next was enough to make most travelers scramble to shore and run screaming into the heart of the forest. A prehistoric-looking reptile with a foot-long jaw slipped with startling speed into the water and headed straight for Juliane. It took willpower, but she kept swimming. She knew that caimans had little interest in attacking humans. It was simply their instinct when threatened to flee into the water, no matter where the threat came from.

As for the other predators, Juliane had the comfort of science on her side. Piranhas, she knew, attack only in stagnant water. If she stuck to the fast-moving current of her river, they would probably leave her alone. Eels take no interest in humans, and the electrical jolt they pack lasts for only two milliseconds. Despite the experience of Humboldt's horses, that was hardly long enough to drown a full-sized human. And the fearsome candiru? Only a couple of cases have been documented in which the spiny beasts had to be removed from a human being.

As she drifted with the current, Juliane felt her confidence return. More often than not, the skies were clogged with storm clouds and gave up no sign of rescue planes. But with the current behind her, she made better progress. She could only hope it was bringing her closer to another human being.

CHAPTER 6

SWARM

B y the end of the week, Juliane could tell she was getting weaker. The candies were long gone. She hadn't eaten solid food since Christmas Eve morning. She'd been drinking murky brown river water for days.

Walking took tremendous effort, and she was happy to let herself drift in the middle of the river. Occasionally, she had to paddle or kick to avoid logs bobbing in her path. Mostly, she treaded water and floated, letting the current carry her. The river water was cool. It did most of the work for her exhausted body. It also gave her relief from the most voracious predators in all the jungle—the bugs.

Every traveler who sets foot in the rainforest complains bitterly about insects. And they don't mean an occasional whining mosquito or tickling ant, but hordes of bugs so dense they make a solid curtain of insect life. Black flies collect in swarms that look like clouds of smoke. "The torments I suffered when skinning a bird or drawing a fish can scarcely be imagined," reported the naturalist Alfred Russell Wallace. "My feet were so thickly covered with the little blood-spots produced by their bites, as to be of a dark purplish-red color and much swelled and inflamed."

Mosquitoes came in numbers so great that early Spanish explorers sometimes labored in pairs, one person swatting bugs so the other could work. Humboldt, the German naturalist, was tormented by the swarming beasts. "[They] cover the face and hands," he reported, "pierce the clothes with their long sucker . . . and, getting into the mouth and nostrils, set you coughing and sneezing whenever you attempt to speak in the open air."

They could also cause a lot more than discomfort. Mosquitoes transmit malaria, a disease that causes intense pain and crippling fevers. Wallace contracted it while he was traveling the Rio Negro in northern Brazil. "During two days and nights I hardly cared if we sank or swam," he recalled later. "I could not speak intelligibly, and had not the strength to write, or even turn over in my hammock."

And then there were the ants, which build their nests everywhere—in the ground, in the bushes, in the trees. When army ants hunt for termites, cockroaches, and other prey, they march from their nest in a column that can fan out 100 feet wide. In some parts of the rainforest, ants outweigh all the vertebrate species combined. And they defend their territory with a vengeance. The naturalist Richard Spruce once wandered into a nest of *tocandira* ants. The tiny creatures swarmed his legs and arms, stinging with abandon. After the attack, Spruce spent hours sick to his stomach, sweating and trembling. "My sufferings," he said, "were indescribable."

Juliane had avoided vast armies of ants so far, but when she wasn't submerged in the water, flying insects tormented her. Mostly, she gave in to the assaults. Swatting at mosquitoes and fanning at black fly swarms served no purpose. Kill one attacker and another replaced it. The insect hordes had an inexhaustible supply of reinforcements, and they left Juliane covered in tiny red welts.

The assorted stings and bites didn't worry her. But when she sat down on the riverbank to inspect her wounds, she discovered something else that made her recoil in horror. The

While they're on the move, army ants make temporary nests out of their own bodies to protect their queen.

cut on her calf had swelled and turned a sickening whitish color. But the truly shocking sight came when she turned her head to examine the cut on the back of her right arm. She had to contort herself to see the wound, and what she saw made her stomach churn: The exposed flesh crawled with tiny white heads.

Flies had been laying their eggs in her wound, just as they had done with the corpses buried in the airplane seats. The brood had hatched, and her body now hosted dozens of hungry maggots, feeding on her flesh.

It was all part of nature's cycle. Flies lay their eggs in places where their larvae can find food. The maggots eat their fill and find a place to pupate. They curl into a hard, protective shell and several days later emerge as a fly.

A natural cycle of life and death, yes—but Juliane did not want to be a part of it. Like most parasites, maggots don't generally kill their host. Still, she had seen what they could do. Her German shepherd, Lobo, once got infested from a tiny cut. The maggots tunneled through his leg until it swelled and began to smell terribly. It was so painful the poor dog wouldn't let anyone near him. Finally, Juliane and her parents coaxed the maggots out by pouring kerosene on the wound.

Juliane had no choice but to try to pick them out, one by one. She used the only tools she could find—the buckle on her watchband and a spiral ring that she unwound into a sharp prod. Neither weapon worked. When she dug in the wound, trying to spear the vile creatures, they wriggled deeper into her flesh and out of reach. She gave up, and a new fear took root: *Even if she was saved, would they have to amputate her arm?*

Each afternoon as the light grew dim, Juliane found a place along the river where she could lean against a sandy bank or a tree trunk. If something truly wanted to attack, a hill or a tree would provide no protection at all. But somehow it felt comforting to have a barrier at her back.

She needed every bit of comfort she could find, because the nights had turned into a 12-hour torment. As she lay down to rest, the jungle came alive around her. Invisible creatures filled the air with rustling and screeching and hammering. Occasionally, something crawled across an ankle or a calf. A tarantula? A snake? The spearhead of an ant attack?

The heat of the day brought some relief from the bugs. But when the sun went down, they came out in force, feasting on every inch of exposed skin. They crawled into her ears and nose and surrounded her head with a constant whining hum.

The only relief from the onslaught came when the skies opened and the rain fell in buckets. The water drove the insects away, but it soaked Juliane to the bone. She collected giant palm leaves and pulled them over her. She tucked herself under bushes or into the crevices of massive tree trunks. But nothing kept her from shivering in the mud, alone and helplessly exposed.

Rainy season in the Peruvian rainforest lasts from December through April. It's not unusual for it to rain, and rain hard, every day. The downpours feed one of the miraculous cycles that create life in the rainforest. A quarter of the water runs off into rivers and streams. The rest soaks into the ground, where trillions of roots drink it in and deliver it up trunks and stems to feed 400 billion trees. The trees consume another quarter of the water and use it for growth. The rest evaporates from the leaves into the sky, where it fills the clouds until they release it once again in buckets to the earth, and the water cycle begins anew.

It's a process that sustains one of the most beautiful, rich, and diverse ecosystems on Earth. But it leaves a path of destruction

Floodwaters threaten a mountain village near Cuzco.

in its wake. "Cities and towns flood," says the naturalist and explorer Paul Rosolie, "dirt roads become muddy rivers, and actual rivers can swell more than fifty feet in places, exploding far onto land. Larger tributaries can burst their banks and flood miles of forest, ripping thousands of trees from the earth in the all-encompassing current."

Yossi Ghinsberg, the Israeli backpacker who got lost in Bolivia, was caught in a massive flood as he tried to follow a river to safety. One minute he'd been standing on dry land; the next he was wading through chest-deep water. He stumbled from tree to tree to keep the current from sweeping him away.

The flood followed a vicious storm that had descended on Ghinsberg the night before while he huddled under a shelter of vines and palm fronds. The water turned solid ground into mud in an instant. Giant trees toppled with a deafening roar, taking smaller trees with them as they fell. The jungle seemed like a living being to Ghinsberg, trying to crush him because he had intruded. "It's the only thing that will pacify this jungle, let it settle peacefully back into its former calm," he wrote later. "It wants to expel this arrogant interloper, this man who dared to think he could survive here alone."

Juliane had not deliberately challenged the jungle. She had not been arrogant—unless it was arrogance to think that humans could fly like birds over the trees. She had been dropped by chance into this waterlogged forest. She had been abandoned by everyone and everything she knew.

That was the feeling that came over her at night, when the wind shook the trees and the sky opened like a faucet. It was then, cowering on the forest floor through the intolerable nights, that her mind wandered over what had happened. She wondered where her mother was. *Had she been rescued by a patrol? Lifted from the forest by a helicopter?* Always the image of the three bodies, buried upside down in the mud, hovered at the edge of her mind. And vaguely she held two thoughts together without resolving them. She knew it was nothing short of a miracle she had survived and wondered why she would be the one. At the same time, she assumed that others had made it through and that one of those survivors was her mother.

———◈———

One day, Juliane swam ashore, found a patch of sun, and lay down to rest. By now, she had lost track of time. *Had New Year's Eve come and gone already?* Her mother had wanted so badly to be home in Panguana, celebrating with her father.

As she dozed on the sandy bank, a familiar squawk woke her with a start. Several baby caimans, less than a foot long, lay on the sand—far too close for comfort. The babies themselves were no danger, but their mother could be vicious if she felt her nest was threatened.

An instant later, a full-grown female rose on her stubby legs and came straight at Juliane's resting place. With a burst of adrenaline, Juliane made it to the water and plunged in. The

The yacare is one of the smaller caimans, but it can still grow as big as a rowboat.

caiman stayed on the riverbank, content to defend her territory. Juliane drifted away, reminded yet again that she was an intruder in a world that was not her own.

For days now, something about the river had been eating away at her confidence. She had seen more wildlife than she was used to around Panguana. In addition to the caimans, howler monkeys and small brocket deer lingered near the shore. One night a paca—a rodent the size of a small coyote—came nosing around her bed.

These animals had not yet learned to be afraid of people— and it wasn't because they were stupid. Most likely they had never seen another human being. If that was true, this river that was her only link to civilization could be uninhabited for miles around. No matter how hard she tried to survive, rescue might be nothing more than a dream.

LOSING HOPE

There were chickens, she was sure of it—and chickens did not run wild in the rainforest. She heard them clucking and knew she'd been saved. Just through the trees there must be a riverside village where people raised birds for eggs and meat. They would take her in and feed her soup. They would put her in a boat and bring her to a doctor, to her father, maybe even to her mother.

But when she looked around, she saw nothing but forest.

Again and again as she made her way down the river she heard the chickens, always just out of sight. Each time, she thought the ordeal had come to an end—the swimming and the walking; the mosquitoes and the black flies; the cold, wet nights; and the deep, unbearable loneliness.

But each time, when she stopped to look for a person tending a manioc field or bathing in the river, the fantasy vanished. The "chickens" were a wild forest bird, or another animal, or the sound of raindrops landing on the river. They were a creation of her own brain, starving for nourishment and desperate for the sight of another human being.

By her second week in the forest, Juliane was failing fast. Starvation had drained her strength and made her mind unreliable. She didn't feel particularly hungry, and that puzzled her. But when the human body is starved for food it protects itself by lowering its need for fuel. Days ago she had burned through the stores of fat in her cells. Now her body harvested protein from its muscles to keep itself alive. Her brain consumed its own neurons.

When she lay down at night and tried to get comfortable, she dreamed of food—giant, mouthwatering dinners and simple snacks. Each time she rested it took a tremendous effort to stand up again. In the water, she used all her strength to get through the maze of drifting logs without breaking a bone or hitting her head.

She knew she had to eat in order to keep going. But she had no idea how to get food. On first glance, the rainforest looks like the most fertile place on Earth. Surely an environment that produces towering trees and lush vegetation should offer up nuts and fruits and edible plants around every river bend. But in fact, the giant trees soak up most of the nutrients in the soil. Plants that grow below the canopy have to compete bitterly with one another to survive. The species that make it are the ones that defend themselves with thorns and spines or poisonous chemicals. Few of them produce anything to eat.

The real bounty of the forest lay in the canopy, 100 feet above Juliane's head. Aguaje fruit, brazil nuts, acai berries, and figs flourish in the treetops. But they might as well have been dangling from the search planes that taunted Juliane from the sky. When Yossi Ghinsberg began to starve in the Bolivian Amazon, he spent hours throwing rocks at fruit that mocked him from the tops of the trees. "I couldn't bear the thought that I might die of hunger while mountains of fruit hung over my head, out of my reach," he wrote. "It wasn't fair. Who was all the fruit for?"

Yossi Ghinsberg was finally rescued after three weeks alone in the rainforest.

Stuck on the forest floor, Juliane had few options. With a machete she could have chopped through palm stalks and eaten the core. With a blowgun and years of training, she could have picked off a bird in the trees. With fishhooks, she could have pulled a bass or a catfish out of the river. But without tools, the forest was barren to her.

The only animals she could imagine catching were the frogs. In the rainy season, they were everywhere, hopping in the sand and mud, oblivious to the desperate human that shared their riverbank. They were gaudy creatures—vibrant yellow and red and blue. The boldest of them were toxic, Juliane knew that; the indigenous people of the Amazon used a fluid from the frogs to poison the tips of their darts.

But most species didn't carry enough poison to kill a person. And the little amphibians were so tempting. They hopped inches from her face as she lay in the sand trying to muster the will to move on. Juliane swiped at them again and again. Each time they darted away before she could get a grasp, and another day went by without an ounce of food to eat.

At night, when there were no vines to battle or logs to dodge, when the problem of where to place a foot or how to stay afloat did not fill her mind—sometimes then, in the dark, she prayed. Her parents didn't believe in a god, exactly. They were scientists, and whatever spiritual beliefs they held came from the forest that towered above Juliane. The sun sustains all life on Earth, and the process it sets in motion inspired a kind of awe in Hans and Maria Koepcke that no

Several species of Amazonian poison frog give off a substance that humans use to poison their hunting darts.

god could match. And still, Juliane prayed—for her mother, for her own rescue, for some kind of human contact.

She also started to think about her life in a way she had never done before. What, after all, had she done with her 17 years? She was calm and even-tempered, shy in big groups but happy and comfortable with her good friends. No matter where her parents took her—Germany, Lima, or Panguana—she adapted. She read a lot and did well in school.

She'd had an unusual childhood, with all the research trips and the years dodging snakes and caimans at Panguana. But she also liked doing normal things—going to movies and hanging out with friends. Before she left Lima, her friend Edith had been teaching her volleyball. She'd been looking forward to coming back and going to the beach in a new blue bikini.

She hadn't questioned any of it before. Now, a world apart from beaches and volleyball nets, she found herself asking what it all meant. It was a perfectly acceptable life, but she didn't stand out in any way. She'd been walking the Earth for 17 years and hadn't left a mark. Now that she had fallen from a plane and survived, life felt like a gift she couldn't afford to squander.

What that meant, exactly, she didn't know. She had always loved animals and assumed she would study biology like her parents, but it no longer seemed like enough. She wanted to do something that would make the world a better place—for humans and for the plants and animals that surrounded her.

First, she had to get out of the forest. She wanted it more than ever, but her body was so weak. Her arm, infested with maggots, throbbed with pain. It was all she could do each morning to stagger to her feet and drag herself to the water. And in the days since she had found the river, she had observed nothing to make her think she would ever see another human being again.

⎯⎯◈⎯⎯

On Sunday, January 2, 1972, as the afternoon light dimmed, Juliane struggled out of the river and collapsed onto the bank. She'd been walking, wading, and swimming for nine days without food. In minutes she was dozing on her back in the gravel. As she drifted in and out of sleep, something at the edge of the water caught her eye. At first it registered only as a thing that did not belong, an object that was not tree, river, or animal. She tried to bring it into focus, and it finally took shape.

It was a boat.

At least it looked like a boat.

She blinked and rubbed her eyes. Each time she looked, it was still there. But she couldn't make herself believe it was real. In a week and a half she'd seen just three things made by human hands—two banks of seats and an engine, each of them ripped from the LANSA flight in midair. They were fossils, reminders that the entire world she once inhabited had deserted her. If her starving brain wasn't playing tricks on her, this was a functional boat used by living human beings. It meant that the world still existed.

She dropped into the water and swam. She had to put her hands on it to be sure it was real. When she got there, she knew: It was not a log masquerading as a boat or a relic abandoned by a hunter decades ago. Floating in her river and tied to the bank by a strand of cable was a brand-new boat, in perfect working condition. And now she took in the entire scene. How could she have missed it? A path led from the boat up the riverbank, and in it she could make out the footprints of another human being.

CHAPTER 8

"MY NAME IS JULIANE"

It was just a thin trail through the riverside vegetation, no more than 20 feet long. But Juliane had so little strength left, it seemed to take hours to drag herself to the top. When she reached the flat ground above the riverbank she saw it—a simple shelter, known as a *tambo* by Peruvians. It stood about 10 feet by 15 feet with no walls, a floor of palm bark, and a set of poles holding up a roof of palm leaves. The boat's outboard motor rested on a corner of the floor, along with a can of gasoline, a length of hose, and a plastic tarp.

Behind the shelter, the path continued into the woods. It led, no doubt, to a village full of people, a dirt track that led to a larger village, a road that led to a city and the rest of the world. The sight was so vivid, such a contrast to the emptiness of the last 10 days, that she expected the owner of the boat to appear any minute.

When a few minutes passed and Juliane was still alone, her mind settled on the gas can. The condition of her arm frightened her, the maggots burrowing deeper into her flesh by the minute. If kerosene had drawn the revolting creatures out of her dog's leg, gasoline should work just as well on her arm.

She sat by the gas can and labored to unscrew the cap—the simplest of tasks took all her strength. When it finally came off, she used the piece of hose to suck up some gas and trickle it into her wound. A red-hot current of pain ran through her arm. In a minute, the wriggling white heads surfaced in her flesh. She took off her spiral ring, unwound it, and picked out the maggots, one by one. She counted 30 of them before she stopped, exhausted from the effort.

By now, the daylight filtering through the trees had faded. No one had appeared on the path behind the shelter.

Resigned to another night alone, Juliane lay down and tried to sleep. But consoling as it was to rest in a real human habitation, she couldn't get comfortable. She had lost weight, and the bark floor bit into her hips and her back. After 10 days yearning for a roof over her head, she stepped out from under the palm leaves and found a place again on the soft riverbank.

This time, she carried a plastic tarp with her. She climbed under it and pulled it over her head. She shut out the mosquitoes, the black flies, and the rain, and slept through the night.

———◈———

When Juliane woke, the questions and the doubts returned. Someone would come eventually to use the boat—but when? The shelter could be an outpost on the far edge of someone's hunting or logging territory. It could be weeks before the owner came back to it. Maybe she should get back in the river and move on.

All morning, the options drifted in and out of her mind. It occurred to her that she could launch the boat and try to ride the river to civilization. But could she really navigate the logs and the current when she could barely stand on her own? And suppose she saved herself by stealing a boat and left someone else stranded in the forest to die. She couldn't bring herself to do it, no matter how desperate she was.

She let the hours slip past like river water. Around noon, the sky darkened and the clouds opened. The drenching rains were a daily ritual by now. She pulled the tarp close around her and sat in the shelter, numb and unable to decide what to do.

When the rain let up, she made a feeble attempt to catch frogs. Hunger wasn't so much an urge as a problem to solve. If she decided to move on, she needed strength, and starvation had left her exhausted to the core. If she stayed, she might have to stay alive for days or weeks before anyone came, and she knew she wouldn't last long without food.

In the afternoon, she finally decided to get back in the river and swim. But now that she had made up her mind, she couldn't bring herself to move. The empty shelter made of rainforest trees was an oasis in the desert. It was the only sign of human civilization she had seen in so long. How could she trade it for the cold desolation of the river? She had the strength to get up again and try to catch frogs. But she couldn't get in the water and leave the shelter behind.

Once again, she felt as though the entire world had abandoned her. The other survivors, she thought, had all been rescued. Only she had been left in the wilderness to starve to death. At some point they would find her body, and no one would know that she had survived a fall strapped to her seat, that she had found a trickle of water and followed it until it became a stream and then a river, that she had stayed alive alone in the forest for this long.

Tomorrow, she told herself—tomorrow, she would get up and she would keep following the river.

By Monday, Peruvians were close to abandoning the search for survivors of the LANSA crash. Newspapers were starting to lose interest in the story because every day the news sounded the same. A rumor would send a new ripple of hope through the exhausted crowds holding vigil at the airports. If the weather allowed, planes took off and ground patrols headed into the jungle. At the end of the day, they came back with the same disheartening message: No sign of Flight 508.

Every flicker of optimism, it seemed, had been snuffed out. Farmers had supposedly seen the plane spinning wildly in the sky 35 miles north of Pucallpa. A priest had seen it 150 miles *south* of Pucallpa. A forest worker had found a "strange thing" half buried in mud 30 miles southwest of Pucallpa. On Monday, in its lone article about the crash, *La Prensa* reported: "All rumors . . . have been dismissed by the search command."

A spokesman for the command insisted they weren't giving up the search. A U.S. Air Force Hercules C-130 plane was on its way with state-of-the-art cameras and other equipment. But that day, while Juliane waited at the shelter, only two planes went up to search for survivors. The search commander, Teddy del Carpio, sounded like he was ready to admit defeat. "It'll take a miracle for us to find the plane," he said.

A relative of Narda Sales Rios, the singer who'd been on Flight 508 with her five-year-old son, told a reporter, "The

jungle has swallowed the plane, and when that happens the jungle does not give anything back."

———◈———

In Juliane's corner of the jungle, dusk fell. She readied herself for a second night at the shelter. Then, with the light fading and the swollen river rushing below, she heard what sounded like human voices.

They couldn't be voices, she thought. How many times had she heard the chickens and believed she'd been saved, only to have her hopes crushed by the sound of the birds and the monkeys and the frogs? It had to be the forest, conspiring with her brain to fool her again.

But the voices grew louder and they mingled with footsteps, and as the thought formed in her mind that these were real people from the real world, three men stepped out of the forest and stood, staring through the open walls of the shelter with shock and even fear in their faces.

She spoke in Spanish. "I'm a girl who was in the LANSA crash," she said. "My name is Juliane."

CHAPTER 9

SURVIVOR

Beltrán Paredes, Carlos Vásquez, and Nestor Amasifuén could barely believe their eyes. The three forest workers never encountered strangers near the *tambo*—especially not white people. Paredes froze with fear for a moment. He thought Juliane might be the incarnation of a water spirit that was said to have blond hair and fierce powers. According to tradition, if a pregnant woman looked the spirit in the eye, she would lose her child.

"It's a good thing you spoke to us right away," Paredes said.

It was also extremely lucky the men were there in the first place. They often spent nights in the forest on trips to hunt or cut wood, but rarely did they come check on the boat. They hadn't been planning to visit the *tambo*, but Amasifuén had talked the others into it. The weather looked bad, and he wanted to have a roof over his head.

If they hadn't changed their plans, Juliane might never have been found. The river that flows past the *tambo*, they told her, is called the Shebonya. As she had feared, no one lived along its banks for miles in either direction.

Juliane could tell the men were worried about her. She looked a mess, skinny and weak with the zipper of her filthy dress broken in the back. The forest floor had been battering her feet for ten days. Her collarbone poked unnaturally at the skin near her neck. Her shin and her arm hosted open wounds, swollen and white and infested with parasites.

The men laid a blanket on the bark floor and sat Juliane down. They gave her some farinha, which she could barely choke down. The pasty gruel of manioc flour and water tasted sour, and she picked at it just to be considerate. While she tried to eat, they turned their attention to her wounds. Juliane had just removed more than two dozen maggots, but when they went to work with the gasoline, dozens more surfaced.

While the men picked parasites from her flesh, Juliane carried on her first conversation since she had sat next to her mother on the plane.

"What about the other passengers?" she asked. "Were they rescued?"

The men were silent for a minute, reluctant to answer.

Finally, Nestor Amasifuén spoke. "No, señorita," he said, "not even the airplane has been found. It has simply disappeared in the jungle, as if it closed its fist around it. As far as I know you are the only survivor."

Juliane spoke near-perfect Spanish, and yet she had trouble

making sense of the words. *How could she have been the only one?* All this time she had assumed there were others, because how could only one person out of 92 survive? And slowly the full meaning of Nestor Amasifuén's words became clear. If it was true that no one else had survived, then her mother too must be dead.

She tossed and turned on the floor of the *tambo* that night. Two other forest workers had arrived seeking shelter from the rain. How strange to have been alone for so long and now to sleep crowded into a space with five other people. The bark floor was hard, and her wounds throbbed from the probing and the gasoline. But the men had given her new clothes and their only mosquito net. She didn't want to insult them by moving to the riverbank.

The next morning, they carried her to the water and laid her in the boat. Marcio Rivera and Amado Pereira, the two new arrivals, nosed the boat into the river she had started following a week ago. They wove in and out of floating logs, and for once she did not have to strain to stay afloat. For hours, she drifted in and out of sleep. The Shebonya emptied into a larger river, the Pachitea. The Pachitea led to a riverbank cleared by human hands and a town of simple houses with grass roofs.

It was 4 p.m. when they docked at the village of Tournavista. Their arrival drew a crowd. People stared as though Juliane were a strange new species, emerging from the jungle for the first time. She and the two men had stopped at a riverside farm along the way for food, and the children there had run screaming when they saw her. The tiny blood vessels around her pupils had burst, the men told her, probably from the change in air pressure as she fell from the plane. Her eyes were no longer white but a shocking, bloody red.

After a week and a half of total solitude, she found herself surrounded. They wanted her on a stretcher, which annoyed her because she could still walk. Someone handed her a bathrobe, and someone else took a picture. A nurse examined her and injected her with antibiotics, and before she knew it a missionary pilot stood in front of her asking if she was ready to get back on a plane. Forty miles away, at the missionary community in Yarinacocha, she would have privacy and expert medical attention.

She didn't have the strength to argue.

The flight to Yarinacocha proved to be the second-most frightening plane ride of Juliane's life. The pilot insisted she lie down, which made it worse. The tiny twin-engine plane banked hard into turns, and Juliane had no way to confirm that they weren't headed for another fiery crash into the rainforest.

After twenty minutes of terror, she was delivered safely to the Summer Institute for Linguistics. The community there was deep in mourning for the five members they had lost to the LANSA crash. The pilot Floyd Lyon had given up hope for his son, who had waited in line for Flight 508 with Juliane. Pat Davis had decided she would continue her work in Peru

Nathan Lyon (top) and the Hedges family (bottom): Margery and Roger with their kids, Rebecca and Timothy.

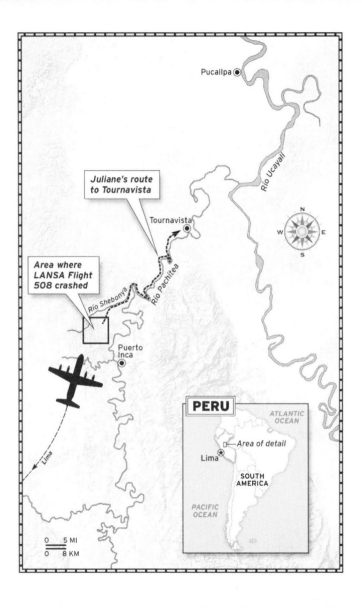

Juliane followed the Shebonya River to the forest shelter. From there she was taken by boat to the Pachitea and then on to Tournavista.

without her husband, Harold, who was also on the plane. Rebecca and Timothy Hedges, who were just seven and five years old, were still recovering from chicken pox. Their illness had kept them in Yarinacocha while their parents, Roger and Margery, traveled to Lima for a visa and then boarded Flight 508 to come home to their kids.

For now, no one overwhelmed Juliane with questions. A doctor named Frank Lindholm took her in. He treated her wounds, pulled more maggots out of her flesh, and extracted a huge wooden splinter from her foot. When he finished, Juliane ate a chicken sandwich—the first food she had actually enjoyed in nearly two weeks. Then she lay down in a large, soft, dry bed and slept.

———————◆———————

Bob Weninger, the missionary pilot from Wisconsin, flew into Pucallpa at around 5 p.m. that night. He had spent four or five days searching for the LANSA wreckage before he had to return to his regular duties. When he landed at Pucallpa and climbed down from the cockpit, he saw the aircraft manager running across the tarmac. "Roberto! Roberto!" he was yelling. "They found a girl!"

Weninger flew to Tournavista that night and told Commander del Carpio that this time he was going to find the plane. It had to be within two minutes' flying time of the forest shelter, he figured. He tracked down Amado Pereira and Marcio Rivera and made them promise to guide him to the shelter.

The next morning, a thick fog shrouded the forest. In Pucallpa, the search pilots waited, convinced there was no point in taking off. In Tournavista, Weninger had no patience for waiting. He ushered the two forest workers into his red-and-white twin-engine Cessna and rose above the fog.

By the time they neared the shelter, the sky below was clearing. Weninger followed the Shebonya River upstream and told Pereira and Rivera to watch for vultures lurking in the treetops.

In a minute or two, Weninger figured he had flown too far south. He turned around, and within seconds, they spotted a crumpled hunk of fuselage cradled in the tree limbs below. As he circled low, the men scanned the canopy, and other foreign objects appeared in the branches. Suitcases, clothes, and packages clung to the trees, the first sign that nearly two weeks ago, 92 people had disappeared into the forest.

Juliane woke on Wednesday, January 5, in the embrace of a real bed. It took a few moments to remember why she was there. When the details came back to her, she felt strangely numb. She had come as close to death as possible and survived—but she did not feel overjoyed to be alive. She had lost the person she loved most—but she did not feel devastated. The crash and the days in the jungle and the rescue and the passengers who had vanished—when she thought about it all she felt nothing.

It still seemed impossible that 91 people had been with her one minute and were gone the next. In the forest, she hadn't let herself think they could be dead. Maybe all along she had been protecting herself from the thought that her mother was gone.

Had she thought about it rationally, it should have seemed obvious. The airplane seat was Juliane's only source of protection during her fall from the plane. And she knew her mother had been ejected from the seat before it hit the ground.

Still, Juliane had believed that Maria was safe—and maybe that belief saved her in the end. Maybe it was the only thing that made her get up each morning, get back in the cold water, and swim a mile closer to the riverside shelter.

Now she had finally accepted it: Her mother was not coming out of the jungle alive. But she still felt numb—an emotional deadness that often plagues survivors after a traumatic experience. The part of the brain responsible for generating emotion turns off in order to shut out the full impact of the ordeal. For a time, it's as though you can only touch the world with gloves on your hands.

Juliane was resting at the Lindholms' house, lost in that emotional fog, when the door to her room opened and her father walked in.

"How are you doing?" he asked.

"Good," she said.

Then he hugged her and sat down on the bed. It would take a long time before he could bring himself to ask when

Maria Koepcke and young Juliane on an expedition in the rainforest.

Juliane had last seen her mother. He had never been one to talk a lot, and that was fine with Juliane.

In a few hours, her body would give in to the trauma of the last two weeks. For several days, she would run a high fever before finally starting on a full recovery.

In the meantime, she rested in a house with walls that shut out the rain and the sun, the spiders and the black flies, the eerie sounds at night and the rushing water by day—a place where she could sit in silence with her own father close enough to touch.

THE STORY

The letters came in bunches from around the world—the United States and Germany; Costa Rica, New Zealand, and Burundi. Some had no more than two lines for an address:

Juliane Koepcke

Peru

Somehow they found their way to Yarinacocha, and Juliane read them while she recovered.

Schoolkids were especially fascinated by her story. They drew pictures of her in the forest, standing next to fragments of a plane. Young wildlife enthusiasts wanted to know what stingrays were like or if jaguars had gone extinct.

Some people offered their help. A doctor wrote with advice on treating a broken collarbone. A woman who had lost her seventeen-year-old daughter invited Juliane to live with her in Texas. Teenaged boys and young men pledged to be there for her until their dying days. An artist wanted to sculpt her in bronze.

Then there were the wacky—sometimes disturbing—letters. One woman insisted that her soul had kept Juliane company in the forest and led her to safety. Another claimed to have discovered an astronomical reason for Juliane's survival: a triangular pattern formed by Venus, Saturn, and Pluto at the end of December.

Most of the letter writers seemed honestly moved by Juliane's ordeal. They wrote to offer sympathy and to let her know she wasn't alone.

Juliane felt touched by the attention. She also felt unsettled. Her story had been private for 10 days while she wandered alone in the forest. Now the entire world wanted details.

Journalists from around the globe poured into Pucallpa. Teddy del Carpio, commander of the search operations, did what he could to keep them away. He told the press that Juliane was at a hospital when she was still recovering in a private home. He posted guards in Yarinacocha.

Denied access to Juliane, reporters pried the story out of anyone they could find. They talked to the nurse from Tournavista. They tracked down the men who'd found Juliane at the shelter.

When facts weren't available, some reporters settled for rumors. In one account, Juliane had built a raft from forest wood and vines and used it to float down the river. Another reporter gave a melodramatic version of her first encounter with the forest workers. Supposedly, Juliane had gathered the strength to say, "There are dead people!" and then passed out.

Juliane had lost control of her story, and she found it frustrating when it was told wrong. But the mistakes were almost easier to accept than the praise. Every story hailed her survival as a great achievement. "Miracle in the jungle!" proclaimed *La Nueva Crónica*. A columnist called her "a modern heroine." Letter writers told her she'd been "coolheaded" and "fearless."

She did not feel like a hero. Nor did she feel especially brave. That was a word meant for people who deliberately risked their lives. She had only been trying to save herself. And nothing about the experience felt like a miracle. If God had anything to do with her survival, then why was her mother dead? What kind of divine being would let 91 people perish and save only one seventeen-year-old girl?

———◆———

On January 8, an amphibious Twin Otter plane settled onto the runway at the Pucallpa airport, less than 5 miles from Juliane's hideaway at Yarinacocha. Its doors opened, and workmen hauled seven black plastic bags out of the plane. The first of the LANSA flight's 91 victims had come home to Pucallpa.

For the grieving families, this was the beginning of the end. For two weeks they had watched search planes return from their rounds with no news at all. Now they had evidence that could not be denied.

After Bob Weninger first spotted the wreckage, the search turned into a recovery operation. Patrols got as close as they could by river and then cut through the forest to the crash site. A helicopter lowered a team through the trees to clear a landing area.

The rainforest did not give up its quarry easily. As Juliane thought, the plane had been torn apart nearly 4,000 feet above the canopy. Its wreckage had rained down across 5 square miles of forest.

As the patrol members picked their way through the disaster area, it was the personal belongings they noticed. Purses, shirts, and sweaters hung from the trees. Watches, photos, gifts, and shoes—dozens of shoes—lay strewn around the forest floor. A doctor who was called to the scene later recalled that

A soccer ball, a child's shoe, and some clothes found among the wreckage.

"suitcases had opened in midair and the presents hung in the branches as if these were Christmas trees decorated for a sad, holy night."

The first bodies were found inside a large piece of the fuselage. Workers had to use an axe to hack their way into the cockpit. They emerged with the body of the pilot, Carlos Forno Valera.

Fernando Ribeiro, who had joined a civilian patrol, identified his fourteen-year-old daughter, Elizabeth, by the gold earrings he had given her. Ribeiro insisted on carrying her remains himself from the wreckage to a waiting helicopter.

The helicopter lifted the bodies to the nearby town of Puerto Inca, where officials had set up a staging area. Relatives waited there or in Pucallpa to identify the remains. A brother recognized his sister's shoes—white with cork soles. An uncle knew his nephew from a bandage on his right leg.

By noon on Saturday, four days after Juliane arrived in Tournavista, half the bodies had been recovered. Eventually, the remains of all 91 passengers and crew would be lifted from the jungle.

Among the items recovered from the forest was Flight 508's black box, which recorded all conversations in the cockpit and any instructions sent from the pilots to the plane's electronic systems. Investigators studied its contents to find out what had happened during the final minutes of the flight. "Catastrophic disintegration in the air" were the words they used to describe the disaster. The lightning strike and severe turbulence had

A piece of the Electra's tail (top) and a row of seats (bottom) just like the one that carried Juliane from the disintegrating plane to the ground.

ripped the wings off the fuselage. Under pressure, the rest of the plane broke into pieces.

There were also signs that the pilot had played a role. Carlos Forno Valera may have panicked, fighting to keep the plane level when he should have let it ride the storm.

The report made no judgment about the fitness of the plane. But the investigators who had looked into the earlier LANSA crash in Cuzco had not been happy with the airline's maintenance crew. Many of the mechanics were new to aviation. They had never fixed anything more complicated than motorcycles.

Juliane's father wanted to hold LANSA responsible for the crash. But when he tried to sue the airline, he got nowhere. The Electra that carried 91 people to their deaths had been the company's last plane. With no money and no assets, LANSA had been shut down for good.

The accident report also said nothing about how Juliane could have survived a lengthy fall from a disintegrating plane. Juliane would eventually come up with her own explanation. She remembered her seat spinning through the sky, which could have created a helicopter effect that slowed her descent. Intense storms can also create updrafts of air that might have cushioned the seat on its way down. The thick forest canopy and its tangle of vines probably did the rest of the work.

Late in January, while the recovery efforts were winding down, doctors declared Juliane healthy enough to travel. She and her father left Yarinacocha for the peace and quiet of Panguana. But even there, they couldn't hide from a curious world. One day, a nurse arrived at the door, claiming that she'd been sent to examine Juliane. When Juliane recognized the "nurse" as a reporter from Yarinacocha, Hans Koepcke ushered the woman out the door.

All Juliane wanted now was to go back to Lima and be a normal teenager. She still had two years of school left before she could take her *Abitur*, the final exams that would qualify her for college. Then she would go to a university in Germany. In the meantime, she'd hang out with her friends, get ice cream, go to the beach, and study. She would leave the plane crash behind and move on.

But when she left Panguana to board a plane in Pucallpa, "normal" seemed like a dream. Journalists mobbed her at the airport, shouting their questions: *Juliane, have you recovered? Juliane, what are you going to do now?* Photographers snapped pictures of her arriving in Lima. Ordinary Peruvians came up to her in the street. They asked for autographs or simply wanted to touch her.

Juliane still wanted to stay and reclaim her life. But her father had seen enough. He bought her a plane ticket for Germany and arranged for her to live with her aunt. At the airport, Juliane waved at the photographers. She swallowed her fear of flying again and boarded a plane for the long flight across the Atlantic.

In 20 harrowing minutes over the Peruvian rainforest, her life had been torn apart. It was time to put the pieces back together.

Reporters besiege Juliane at the Lima airport as she gets ready to leave for Germany.

EPILOGUE

PAYBACK

n 1977, Juliane stepped off a plane in Lima for the first time since the LANSA crash. A crowd of journalists heard she was coming and tracked her down, asking for interviews. But she wasn't there to relive the crash.

She had come back to study butterflies.

After returning to Germany in 1972, Juliane decided to take on the work her parents had loved. She went to university to become a zoologist and study the plants and animals of the rainforest.

Her ordeal in the forest still haunted her. The flying nightmare that seized her the night of the crash returned again and again. Sometimes she dreamed that her mother was still alive, standing on the other side of a street. In the dream, Juliane ran across the street, ecstatic and relieved. But just after she fell into her mother's arms, she woke up.

It took several years before she let herself truly feel the loss. One Christmas Day, it finally hit her. "I cried for hours and hours, all day long, almost without end," she recalled years later, "and thought of my mother and all the important subjects I didn't discuss with her."

Had Maria Koepcke lived, she and her daughter would have found plenty to talk about. On that visit in 1977, Juliane spent a month in Panguana, catching and observing butterflies, and rediscovering the rainforest she had loved as a kid.

Four years later, she returned to study bats. She slept in a hut without walls, draped by a mosquito net. She learned to butcher wild pigs, cook caiman tails, and use herbal medicine to cure toothaches. She went out under the moonlight with the Milky Way shining overhead. She probed inside hollow trees to observe bat colonies. She surprised an ocelot one night and a jaguar another.

Juliane got to know the forest the way her parents knew it, as a student of the sights and sounds, the complicated relationships between animals, trees, and plants. "I took in the forest with all my senses," she later wrote, "the endless diversity of the vegetation and wildlife and their adaptations, nature's incredible play of colors . . . the sounds that sometimes enveloped me like a cloak and that always give me pleasure to this day, the smells, the green and yellow twilight, the warm dampness of the forest."

On her midnight explorations, Juliane discovered the "secret soul" of the Amazon. "I felt as if I were plunging into the energy of a powerful, all-embracing living thing, so intimate by now, and yet always unfamiliar in new ways," she wrote.

She had nearly died in the rainforest, hungry and alone. But it did not feel like a "green hell" to Juliane. It was not a

A majestic lupuna tree towers 150 feet over the research station at Panguana.

lair for man-eating caimans and deadly snakes. It was a place of wonder, of awe—a place where she felt safe. The forest, she said, had helped her "return to human life."

During the long, desperate nights she spent huddled in the rain after the plane crash, she had vowed to do something important with her life. Now she knew what that task was. She would devote herself to preserving the little patch of rainforest that gave her and her parents so much joy. *My task has a name,* she thought. *And it is Panguana.*

———◆———

Seventeen years later, in the dry season of 1998, Juliane peered out the window of a helicopter at a vast stretch of forest in Peru. The helicopter settled into a small clearing, not far from the Shebonya River. A balding man in khakis helped her down while a film camera recorded the scene.

The man was Werner Herzog, the movie director who had been desperate to get on the LANSA plane that Christmas Eve in 1971. For nearly three decades he'd been haunted by the crash and the lone girl who had survived. Finally, he had tracked Juliane down in Munich and asked if he could make a documentary about her.

Juliane, now in her forties, had done her best to put the crash behind her. She had married a fellow zoologist and found a job she loved, running the library at one of the largest natural history museums in the world. Reporters still pestered her for interviews from time to time. She turned them all away. But she had seen a couple of Herzog's films and liked them. He would not be like the other journalists, she thought. Maybe it was the right time to revisit the past.

Herzog's crew had made four expeditions into the jungle before they found the plane wreckage. Pieces of fuselage the size of a car had been completely hidden by vines.

Juliane spent a couple of days wandering among the wreckage, telling the story of the crash. She sifted through pieces of debris from the forest floor—a hair curler, the heel of a woman's shoe, a piece of a tray on which the flight attendants served sandwiches just before the plane plunged into the storm. At one point she peered at a window-sized opening in a piece of fuselage. Above the window, the words SALIDA DE EMERGENCIA were still readable—"Emergency Exit."

At first, the experience left Juliane feeling distant, like she herself was watching a movie. That numbness had helped her survive a terrible tragedy when she was seventeen. Three decades later it was still with her. "It's a mechanism that allows us to live with a monstrous experience," she reflected, "to deal with it as if it were a birthmark that belongs to us, a scar, an affliction. Or sometimes even a blessing. Who can decide?"

Before the film crew left the crash site, they stumbled across a massive piece of the plane that lay camouflaged on the forest floor. As they hacked away with machetes, a 40-foot piece of fuselage with its landing gear still intact emerged from the vines and the undergrowth.

Juliane, now forty-three, wanders among the wreckage of the LANSA flight during the filming of *Wings of Hope*.

The sight finally made the memories feel real to Juliane. "Lying there like that," she recalled, "it reminded me terribly of the remains of a dead bird, a real living thing stranded helplessly with its feet pointing upwards." It symbolized something final—as though 30 years after she survived a nearly 4,000-foot fall into the trees, the ordeal was finally over.

———◦———

In 2011, 40 years after the crash, Juliane landed again in Peru. This time, she was ready to finish the mission she had vowed to undertake years earlier. She had come to save a small corner of the rainforest she loved.

Since Flight 508 crashed in the jungle, the Amazon has been under attack by farmers, loggers, miners, and ranchers. It has lost nearly 15 percent of its trees. An area larger than the country of France has been hacked and burned out of the "uninterrupted" wilderness that Richard Spruce marveled at when he first arrived in 1849.

Juliane had noticed the destruction when she came back with Herzog in 1998. A major highway sliced through the edge of the forest from Venezuela through Peru to Bolivia. On either side of the road, acres of trees had been cut down or burned away. Unbroken forest was giving way to a patchwork of cattle ranches, small farms, and smoldering stumps. It looked as though the Amazon was slowly being burned to death.

The rate of deforestation has declined in recent years. But at its worst, the Amazon lost an area the size of 600 football fields every hour—1 square mile gone in the time it takes to brush your teeth.

Highways now cross the rainforest from the east coast of Brazil to the west coast of Peru. Off of those roads, loggers and miners have built 100,000 miles of illegal tracks into remote areas of the forest. Loggers offer woodcutters $30 for a mahogany tree that will eventually sell for $3,000 overseas. Miners come in digging for gold and leave behind house-sized mounds of dirt and rocks.

The most intrusive new residents of the rainforest, though, aren't farmers, loggers, or miners. They're cows—more than 200 million of them. Cattle ranchers are responsible for at least

Massive logs, cut down from the rainforest, await processing at a sawmill near Iquitos.

70 percent of deforestation in the Amazon. They ship nearly 2 million tons of beef overseas every year. Hides from their cows are made into leather for soccer cleats. Fat from the carcasses gets processed into toothpaste and cosmetics.

The desire to make a profit on the forest goes back to Pizarro and the other Europeans who blundered their way into the Amazon in the 16th century. Eventually, the early explorers gave up on El Dorado. But their dream survived—that with energy, willpower, and technological skill, the rainforest could be turned into a source of great wealth. In 1852, an American expedition emerged from the Amazon and reported that the forest was the world's biggest untapped resource. With the right tools, the soil beneath its 400 billion trees could feed the world. Bring "the railroad and the steamboat, the plough, the axe, and the hoe," the expedition's leaders claimed, and the rainforest would produce "power, wealth and grandeur" to rival any empire.

The Amazon hasn't been a lot more hospitable to the plough and the axe than it was to the early explorers. The soil in the rainforest doesn't lend itself well to farming or ranching. Without tree roots to suck up water, storms simply wash the top layer of soil away. With it go most of the nutrients in the soil. Grass and food crops grow well for a couple of years after the forest is cleared. Then the yield drops off. Farmers need to clear even more land. Ranchers have to buy expensive feed to keep their cattle nourished.

Still, the destruction continues, and the consequences are

serious. Indigenous people have been forced off their land by loggers and ranchers. The Awa-Guaja, one of the few nomadic tribes left in the Amazon, nearly went extinct when a third of their land was destroyed. Thousands more indigenous people have had to move to cities in search of jobs.

Deforestation also plays a role in the biggest long-term threat to the Earth: climate change. The trees of the rainforest do an important service to the planet. To grow, they need carbon dioxide—one of the gases produced when we burn fossil fuels such as coal and oil. Carbon dioxide is one of the so-called greenhouse gases that trap the sun's heat near Earth, causing the planet to warm. Trees help to limit the effects of carbon dioxide by sucking it out of the air. When those trees are cut down and burned, they return the planet-warming gas to the atmosphere.

Panguana, with its huts and its majestic 150-foot lupuna tree, was just a tiny fraction of this threatened landscape—460 acres out of 1.3 billion. But to Juliane, it was a vital piece. In that small patch of forest, over 400 species of ants eat the bark and leaves of 500 species of trees. Countless more varieties of insects fill the air. They provide dinner for 350 species of birds, 52 species of bats, 50 species of frogs, and 50 species of various reptiles. Another 280 species of butterflies help spread pollen for at least 500 varieties of plants.

Sometimes, when Juliane talked about her work at Panguana, people would ask what the point was. Why did we need to know how many species of dung beetle inhabit the forest, eating monkey poop and burying the fruit seeds they find in it so new fruit trees can grow?

Because, Juliane would answer, we can't appreciate what we have until we understand what it is. "As long as we regard the rain forest as nothing but a wilderness, a 'green hell,' we're behaving like children setting fire to a heap of money just because they don't know what the paper is worth."

In 2011, Juliane and her husband, Erich Diller, had come back to make sure that no one set fire to Panguana. She had found investors to help buy more land around the research station. With the help of a neighbor named Moro, they expanded Panguana from 460 to 1,730 acres. Then they convinced the Peruvian government to declare it off-limits to development of any kind.

Juliane and Erich flew from Lima to Pucallpa and traveled overland to Panguana, meeting with government officials and signing papers. Juliane had finally decided to tell the story of the crash in her own words. She was writing a book that would be published the following year, called *When I Fell from the Sky*.

As they made their way to Panguana, they found echoes of the crash along the way. In Pucallpa, a tomb holds the remains of more than 50 of the LANSA passengers. On it is a map inscribed in plaster marking Juliane's route out of the forest from the crash site. On the way from Pucallpa to Panguana stands a small roadside market that locals know as "The Door." It's named after a rusted hatchway from the LANSA flight that the owner keeps on display. On the piece of wreckage is written *Juliane's door.*

For Juliane, the rainforest has always felt like a world apart. "In the city," she wrote, "nature is a guest you tolerate: you plant a few trees, put plants in front of the window and keep a pet. Here in Panguana, nature is the host and we are the visitors."

It's a relationship Juliane must feel more keenly than most. At seventeen, she should have plummeted to her death in the rainforest. Instead, it welcomed her and guided her back home. She can't understand why she alone, out of 92, became a guest. But she can work to make her survival mean something in the end.

As she puts it: "I'm trying to save the rainforest that saved my life."

Juliane visited the newly protected wilderness area at Panguana in 2014.

GLOSSARY

caiman: a close relative of the alligator, found in Central and South America

canopy: the top branches of trees that form a sort of ceiling in a forest

fuselage: the main body of an aircraft

manioc: a long, starchy root, also called cassava, that is a basic part of the diet in the Amazon. Manioc grows well in the poor soil of the rainforest.

porter: a person whose job it is to carry baggage or other loads

silt: fine sand or earth carried by moving water

sinuosities: curves or bends

sun bittern: a colorful, long-legged bird found near forest streams in Central and South America

wood rail: a long-legged bird native to Central and South America. Wood rails have a distinctive cackling call.

AUTHOR'S NOTE

When I started research for this book, I was excited about the prospect of interviewing Juliane. But when I tried to contact her in Germany, I was told she was engaged in other projects and couldn't tell her story to me.

That left me wondering whether I should write the book at all. I know from Juliane's memoir that she had a hard time when her story became public. She had no control over how it was told. Reporters got details wrong. They portrayed her in ways she didn't think were accurate.

While Juliane was recovering in Yarinacocha, her father allowed reporters from the German magazine *Stern* to spend a couple of days with her. She was still in shock at the time. Her brain and body were protecting her from the trauma of her mother's death. It's a common state for disaster survivors, but the *Stern* reporters seemed to mistake it for indifference. The article portrayed her as courageous but cold—able to cry over the death of her pet blackbird, but not over her mother.

I had to ask whether I could do better. Could I get the story right without hearing it directly from Juliane? Could I add enough to make it worth telling again?

I had one advantage over the reporters who covered the story 45 years ago: Juliane's memoir, *When I Fell from the Sky*. When the book came out, she finally started giving interviews to reporters. My guess is it still wasn't easy for her. She is a private person who was forced into the public eye by a traumatic experience.

Juliane's book, her interviews, Werner Herzog's documentary, and the multipart *Stern* article published in 1972 became my main sources for her part of the story. But I wanted to tell the story from other points of view as well. How did the massive search for the plane progress? What was happening at the Summer Institute for Linguistics, which had lost five members of its own community in the crash? And who were the other people on the plane? In Pucallpa there's a plaster monument where the remains of more than 50 of the flight's victims are interred. In big letters it reads ALAS DE ESPERANZA, "Wings of Hope." Juliane found the inscription ironic since only one person out of 92 survived: What was hopeful about that? I wanted at least some of the passengers who didn't survive to play a role in the book.

None of this research proved to be easy. The organization that started the Summer Institute for Linguistics still exists, and their archivist tried to put me in touch with people who were there at the time. But those people had lost loved ones in the crash, and they didn't feel comfortable putting their memories in the hands of a writer they didn't know.

Through another missionary organization, I eventually tracked down Bob Weninger, the pilot who first spotted the wreckage of Flight 508. He gave me the name of Doug Deming, who was a pilot at the Summer Institute for Linguistics during the crash. Their accounts, plus some 550 jpegs of articles from Peruvian newspaper archives, helped me piece together the rest of the story.

Most important, I wanted to tell Juliane's story as part of a larger narrative of the Amazon rainforest. That, I think, is the way she understands it. She is part of a long history of outside interaction with the Amazon. For five centuries, people who were not born in the forest have come to it with varied motives. Some exploited it for their own gain. Others wanted mainly to understand it. Some tried to destroy it, and others were destroyed by it.

Juliane nearly died in the forest. And yet, she refuses to think of it as a "green hell." She approaches the rainforest with curiosity, not fear, and that attitude matters. The world's population now numbers about 7.5 billion. It will probably climb to 11 billion by the year 2100. We carve our cities and suburbs and farms out of an ever-shrinking natural world. In Europe, for instance, less than 15 percent of land remains unchanged by humans.

How we think about that land is important. If wilderness— be it dense rainforest, frozen tundra, mid-ocean caverns, or the woods in our backyards—feels foreign and frightening to us, we're more likely to look the other way when it's destroyed to make way for a ranch, a mine, or an oil-drilling platform. Those activities provide resources for a growing population. But at some point, they will exhaust the planet that is our home.

As Juliane says, "nature is the host and we are the visitors." If her story can help inspire that kind of approach to living on Earth, then in my opinion it is worth retelling.

SOURCES

Books

Bennet, Glin. *Beyond Endurance*. New York: St. Martin's, 1983.

Chasteen, John Charles. *Americanos: Latin America's Struggle for Independence*. London: Oxford University Press, 2008.

Cobb, Jerrie. *Solo Pilot*. Sun City, FL: Jerrie Cobb Foundation, 1997.

Cook, Noble David. *Born to Die*. Cambridge: Cambridge University Press, 1998.

Cronin, Paul. *Herzog on Herzog*. New York: Farrar, Straus and Giroux, 2002.

Forsyth, Adrian, and Ken Miyata. *Tropical Nature*. New York: Charles Scribner's Sons, 1984.

Ghinsberg, Yossi. *Lost in the Jungle*. New York: Skyhorse Publishing, 2009.

Gonzales, Laurence. *Deep Survival*. New York: W. W. Norton, 2003.

Grann, David. *The Lost City of Z*. New York: Vintage Books, 2009.

Heaney, Christopher. *Cradle of Gold*. London: Palgrave Macmillan, 2010.

Hemming, John. *Naturalists in Paradise*. London: Thames & Hudson, 2015.

———. *The Search for Eldorado*. London: Michael Joseph, 1978.

———. *Tree of Rivers: The Story of the Amazon*. New York: Thames & Hudson, 2008.

Koepcke, Juliane. *When I Fell from the Sky*. London: Nicholas Brealey Publishing, 2012.

Kricher, John. *A Neotropical Companion*. Princeton, NJ: Princeton University Press, 1997.

Leach, John. *Survival Psychology*. London: Palgrave Macmillan, 1994.

Levy, Buddy. *River of Darkness*. New York: Bantam Books, 2011.

Medina, José Toribio. *The Discovery of the Amazon*. New York: Dover, 1988.

Millard, Candice. *The River of Doubt: Theodore Roosevelt's Darkest Journey*. New York: Doubleday, 2005.

Muir, Wesley. *The Man Who Jumped off Clouds*. Hagerstown, MD: Review and Herald Publishing Association, 2000.

Noyce, Wilfrid. *They Survived: A Study of the Will to Live*. New York: E. P. Dutton, 1963.

Rosolie, Paul. *Mother of God*. New York: HarperCollins, 2014.

Savoy, Gene. *Antisuyo: The Search for the Lost Cities of the Amazon*. New York: Simon and Schuster, 1970.

Smith, Anthony. *Explorers of the Amazon*. Chicago: University of Chicago Press, 1990.

———. *The Lost Lady of the Amazon*. New York: Carroll & Graf, 2003.

Suzuki, David. *The Sacred Balance: Rediscovering Our Place in Nature*. Vancouver: Greystone Books, 2007.

Whitaker, Robert. *The Mapmaker's Wife*. New York: Bantam Dell, 2004.

Willis, Jennifer Schwamm. *Explore: Stories of Survival from Off the Map*. New York: Thunder's Mouth Press and Balliett & Fitzgerald Inc., 2000.

Newspapers and Magazines

I relied heavily on coverage of the crash in three Peruvian newspapers: *La Prensa*, *El Comercio*, and *La Nueva Crónica*. Specific articles are cited in end notes.

Magazine and web sources for details on rainforest ecology, deforestation, and aviation are cited in end notes.

"Ein kam durch," *Stern*, Jan. 16, 1972.

"El Valor de una Vida," César Hildebrandt, *Caretas*, Jan. 14, 1972.

"Lansa Accident and Search Report," *Translation*, April–June 1972, Wycliffe Bible Translators.

"Mit Juliane zurück in den Urwald," Rolf Winter, *Stern*, Feb. 13, 1972.

"She Lived and 91 Others Died," Robert G. Hummerstone, *Life*, Jan. 28, 1972.

"So habe ich überlebt," Juliane Koepcke, *Stern*, Parts 1–3, Jan. 23, 30, Feb. 6, 1972.

"Sole Survivor: The Woman Who Fell to Earth," Sally Williams, *The Telegraph*, March 22, 2012.

Author Interviews

Nicholas Asheshov, journalist living in Peru, Feb. 8, 2016.

Doug Deming, missionary pilot at the Summer Institute for Linguistics, Yarinacocha, Peru. Email correspondance, Sept. 26 and Oct. 16, 2016.

Ed Schertz, missionary pilot, July 2016.

Bob Weninger, missionary pilot for Wings of Hope, July 20, 2016.

Ed Zipser, pilot and professor of atmospheric sciences at University of Utah, July 21, 2016.

END NOTES

Prologue: December 24, 1971

Herzog describes the scene at the airport in his film *Wings of Hope* and in Cronin, *Herzog on Herzog*, 268.

Accident records for the LANSA crashes can be found at the Aviation Safety Network website, http://aviation-safety.net

Only plane left: "Flight International," May 18, 1972, http://flightglobal.com

Electra wing trouble is described in Stuart Lee, "Lockheed Electra: Killer Airliner (Part 2)," cs.clemson.edu

Details on the exchange students aboard Flight 502 are from "99 on Airliner Die in Crash in Peru; 54 Are from U.S.," *New York Times*, Aug. 10, 1970.

"*LANSA se lanza de panza*": Koepcke, *When I Fell from the Sky*, 57.

Rovalino's and Sales Rios's reservations described in "Pasajeros de LANSA; Una Extraña Cita con la Muerte," *La Prensa*, Jan. 2, 1972.

"Don't fly LANSA, brother": "Estudiante Adelantó Viaje que Planeaba Para el Año Nuevo," *La Nueva Crónica*, Dec. 29, 1971.

The trip to Cuzco is described in Koepcke, *When I Fell*, 63.

Juliane describes her time at Panguana in Koepcke, *When I Fell*, 47–53 and beyond.

A friend recalls Juliane's talent for imitating tarantulas in "El Valor de Una Vida," *Caretas*, Jan. 14, 1972.

The prom and the decision to fly on Dec. 24 are described in Koepcke, *When I Fell*, 56–57, 62.

Pumacahua's rebellion is described in Chasteen, *Americanos: Latin America's Struggle for Independence*, 113–115.

Nathan Lyon's plan is described by his mother in "6 Due Burial At Peru Post," *Corpus Christi Caller-Times*, Jan. 12, 1972. Profiles of both boys are in "Lansa Accident and Search Report," *Translation*, April–June 1972, Wycliffe Bible Translators.

Juliane's harrowing description of the flight can be found in Koepcke, *When I Fell*, 63–64. She also describes it in Herzog's *Wings of Hope* while in a window seat flying the same route as Flight 508.

Timeline of Flight 508 is from the accident report, provided by the International Civil Aviation Organization.

Piloting strategies in Amazonian storms are from author interviews with Ed Zipser and Ed Schertz.

Chapter 1: The Green Hell

400 billion trees is from a 2013 study described in "400 billion trees belonging to 16,000 different species grow in the Amazon," UPI, Oct. 21, 2013.

"The largest river": quoted in Hemming, *Tree of Rivers*, 140.

"Of all the marvels": Savoy, *Antisuyo*, 104.

Carletti is quoted in Whitaker, *Mapmaker's Wife*, 56.

Juan and Ulloa are quoted in Whitaker, *Mapmaker's Wife*, 84.

"eyes in their shoulders": quoted in Hemming, *Search for El Dorado*, 173.

Orellana's encounter with the Amazon warriors is described in Levy, *River of Darkness*, 158–162, 168–174.

Myth of El Dorado is discussed in Hemming, *Search for El Dorado*, 97–109, and Levy, *River of Darkness*, 17–22.

"goes about continually covered": Fernandez de Oviedo, quoted in Hemming, *Search for El Dorado*, 97.

The tragic effect of smallpox on indigenous Amazonians is discussed in Hemming, *Tree of Rivers*, 63–65. See Cook, *Born to Die*, 1–14 for a general take on the decimation of Amerindians by disease.

Gonzalo Pizarro's expedition is described in Levy, *River of Darkness*.

"They were so pale": Augustin de Zarate, quoted in Levy, *River of Darkness*, 102.

"Some, contrary to nature": Philip von Hutten, quoted in Hemming, *Search for El Dorado*, 63.

"The reports are false": quoted in Grann, *Lost City of Z*, 11.

European travelers often described the subsistence skills of indigenous Amazonians. The Machiguenga people still use the mildly poisonous barbasco root to fish: "Traditional Fishing With Poison Deployed for Science," *Water Currents* blog, Sept. 24, 2014, nationalgeographic.com. Omagua turtle farmers are discussed in Hemming, *Tree of Rivers*, 57, as are manioc farmers, 25–27. The naturalist Henry Bates got a Yuri native to train him in the use of a blowgun: Hemming, *Naturalists in Paradise*, 122.

"meats, partridges, turkeys, and fish": Carvajal in Medina, *The Discovery of the Amazon*, 175.

See a drawing of a top-hatted European carried on the back of an Indian laborer in Whitaker, *The Mapmaker's Wife*, 141. This was just one indignity in a system known as *mita*, in which indigenous people were taxed so heavily that they were forced to work off their debt in conditions not much different from slavery.

"For a man to eat meat": quoted in Hemming, *Tree of Rivers*, 64. Hemming describes how native communities fled deep into the forest to escape Portuguese slaving expeditions. "Rarely in human history," he says, "has so much damage been done to so many by so few."

"This man knows nothing": quoted in Hemming, *Naturalists in Paradise*, 139.

One-tenth the planet's species: "Amazon," worldwildlife.org

One-fifth the world's river water: "Amazon River," britannica .com; Hemming, *Naturalists in Paradise*.

More than 100 uncontacted groups: see survivalinternational
.org

The story of Bob Nichols was told to me by the British journalist
Nicholas Asheshov, who went to search for Nichols after he
was lost. Asheshov was also one of the few reporters who
was allowed to interview Juliane after the LANSA crash.

Chapter 2: Alone

The account of Juliane's first day in the forest is drawn from
Koepcke, *When I Fell*, 65–67 and 74–76; Herzog, *Wings of
Hope*; and "So habe ich überlebt (How I Survived)," *Stern*,
Jan. 23, 1972. These were the three main sources for Juliane's
part of the story, in addition to interviews Juliane gave in
2012 when her book was published. Juliane is critical of the
Stern articles, so I approached them skeptically. However,
they come from interviews done within two weeks of the
time Juliane emerged from the forest. Herzog's documentary
was made 27 years after the crash, and Juliane's book was
written another 14 years after that.

Trees screen out 95 percent of sunlight: Rosolie, *Mother of God*,
6. Rosolie says of his time soloing in the Amazon: "It is the
most profound loneliness imaginable, as though the rest of
the world had ceased to exist."

The work of leafcutter ants is described in Kricher, *Neotropical
Companion*, 133–135.

"There is a weird gloom": quoted in Hemming, *Naturalists in
Paradise*, 11.

The cutthroat lives of lianas are described in Forsyth and
Miyata, *Tropical Nature*, 47–50.

"Do-nothing sickness" is discussed in Leach, *Survival Psychology*,
43–45; and Gonzales, *Deep Survival*, 196.

"Strange how the shallow little footpath": Savoy, *Antisuyo*, 104.

Chapter 3: Follow the Water

The account of Juliane's second, third, and fourth day in the
forest is based on Koepcke, *When I Fell*, 77–80; Herzog,
Wings of Hope; and "So habe ich überlebt," *Stern*, Jan. 23,
1972.

The scene at the Summer Institute comes from *Translation*,
April–June 1972, Wycliffe Bible Institute; and my interview
with Doug Deming.

"LANSA PLANE LOST": "Se Pierde Avion Lansa: 92 A Bordo,"
La Nueva Crónica, Dec. 25, 1971.

Rumors: "Habría sido localizado el LANSA en una quebrada;
FAP dice que no hay nada," *El Comercio*, Dec. 26, 1971.

"any rumor that has circulated": "Dramática es la Búsqueda
Del Avión que Desapareció," *La Nueva Crónica*, Dec. 26,
1971.

"You can't even carry a brick": "Intenso Drama Viven Familiares
de los 92," *La Nueva Crónica*, Dec. 26, 1971.

Blood drive in Pucallpa is described in "Intensifican en Selva
La 'Operación Rastreo,'" *La Nueva Crónica*, Dec. 26, 1971.

"A distant railway train approaching": quoted in Hemming,
Naturalists in Paradise, 49.

"I had never been so terrified": Ghinsberg, *Lost in the Jungle*, 187.

Where the real dangers lay: Koepcke, *When I Fell*, 71–72. *Stern* quotes seventeen-year-old Juliane as saying, "My parents taught me all about the dangers of the jungle—for example, that the big animals—the ocelots, jaguars, or tapirs—aren't what's dangerous; but rather it's the small animals—the insects, the spiders, ants, flies, and mosquitoes."

The 19th-century naturalist Henry Bates did actually come across a Goliath spider killing two small finches it had caught in its web. Bates tried unsuccessfully to rescue one of the birds. Hemming, *Naturalists in Paradise*, 93.

"If you want to be a biologist": Koepcke, *When I Fell*, 20.

The *Stern* reporters claim Juliane saw other parts of the wreckage, but she writes only about the engine in her memoir.

Chapter 4: No Shortcuts

The account of Juliane's ordeal, from finding the three bodies to discovering the river, is from Koepcke, *When I Fell*, 89–91; Herzog, *Wings of Hope*; and "So habe ich überlebt," *Stern*, Jan. 23 and 30, 1972.

Telephone lines clogged: "Familiares Confían que Alguien se Haya Salvado," *La Nueva Crónica*, Dec. 27, 1971.

Bob Weninger described his search for the LANSA plane to me in a phone interview. See also, "The Twelve Days of Christmas 1971," *Aviation News*, Dec. 1972.

"Will they be orphans now?": *La Nueva Crónica*, Dec. 27, 1971.

"Without a machete": quoted in Grann, *Lost City of Z*, 129.

The spectacle of Isabel Godin's departure is described in Whitaker, *Mapmaker's Wife*, 3–5.

The account of the ill-fated expedition is from Whitaker, *Mapmaker's Wife*, 231–263; and Smith, *Lost Lady of the Amazon*, 103–149.

"By keeping along the river's side": Charles Godin, quoted in Whitaker, *Mapmaker's Wife*, 254.

The unusual hoaztin: "Hoatzin," britannica.com

Chapter 5: The River

Juliane's first days on the river are described in Koepcke, *When I Fell*, 90–92; Herzog, *Wings of Hope*; and "So habe ich überlebt," *Stern*, Jan. 23 and 30, 1972.

Juliane says she felt "boundless anger" when the planes disappeared. "I had no idea that I still had the strength for such feelings." Koepcke, *When I Fell*, 90.

Search stalled: "Mal Tiempo en la Selva Impide Hallar al LANSA," *La Nueva Crónica*, Jan. 2, 1972.

Civilian patrols banned: "Prohiben Más Patrullas En la Selva," *La Prensa*, Jan. 1, 1972.

"It's like looking for a needle": "Nuevos Rumores Circulan en Torno al Paradero del LANSA," *La Nueva Crónica*, Dec. 31, 1971.

Juliane describes her father's journey in Koepcke, *When I Fell*, 24–29.

"When we have really resolved": Koepcke, *When I Fell*, 30.

The enslavement of indigenous people along the Amazon is described in Hemming, *Tree of Rivers*, 58–72, 78–82.

Juan and Ulloa's exaggerated fear of caimans is described in Whitaker, *Mapmaker's Wife*, 84.

"They will rend and devour": quoted in Grann, *Lost City of Z*, 91.

Humboldt's experiment is described in Grann, *Lost City of Z*, 91–92.

The candiru's probably fictitious talents are described in Millard, *River of Doubt*, 164–165 and elsewhere.

According to the *Stern* reporters, Juliane said: "If you step on a stingray, I told myself, it's all over."

Juliane describes her encounters with caimans in Koepcke, *When I Fell*, 97.

The electric eel's two-millisecond jolt is described in "How do electric eels generate a voltage and why do they not get shocked in the process?" scientificamerican.com

The candiru myth is exposed in "Would the candiru fish really eat your genitals?" bbc.com, Jan. 4, 2016.

Chapter 6: Swarm

"The torments I suffered": quoted in Hemming, *Naturalists in Paradise*, 179.

"They cover the face and hands": quoted in Whitaker, *Mapmaker's Wife*, 256.

"During two days and nights": quoted in Hemming, *Naturalists in Paradise*, 181.

The supremacy of ants in the rainforest is described in Forsyth and Miyata, *Tropical Nature*, 104.

"My sufferings were indescribable": quoted in Hemming, *Tree of Rivers*, 148.

Juliane's first battle with maggots is described in Koepcke, *When I Fell*, 93–94; and "So habe ich überlebt," *Stern*, Jan. 23, 1972.

The water cycle is discussed in Kricher, *Neotropical Companion*, 49.

"Cities and towns flood": Rosolie, *Mother of God*, 9.

"It's the only thing": Ghinsberg, *Lost in the Jungle*, 236.

Juliane describes her nighttime torments in Koepcke, *When I Fell*, 92.

Juliane's encounter with the mother caiman is described in Koepcke, *When I Fell*, 96–97. The account in *Stern* mentions only the baby caimans.

Juliane's fear that the river is uninhabited is described in Koepcke, *When I Fell*, 94–95.

Chapter 7: Losing Hope

The "false chickens" are discussed in Koepcke, *When I Fell*, 96–97; and "So habe ich überlebt," *Stern*, Jan. 23 and 30, 1972.

Fantasizing about food: Koepcke, *When I Fell*, 96.

Competition for scarce nutrients in the rainforest is explained in Forsyth and Miyata, *Tropical Nature*, 17–29; and Whitaker, *Mapmaker's Wife*, 258–259.

"I couldn't bear the thought": Ghinsberg, *Lost in the Jungle*, 197.

Chasing frogs is described in Koepcke, *When I Fell*, 97.

Juliane describes her dark nights of the soul in Koepcke, *When I Fell*, 92–93.

Finding the boat is described in Koepcke, *When I Fell*, 97–98; "So habe ich überlebt," *Stern*, Jan. 30, 1972; and Herzog, *Wings of Hope*.

Chapter 8: "My Name Is Juliane"

Juliane's night and day at the shelter are described in Koepcke, *When I Fell*, 98–99; Herzog, *Wings of Hope*; and "So habe ich überlebt," *Stern*, Jan. 30, 1972.

"All rumors have been dismissed": "Dos Aviones Durante 10 Horas Buscaron Al Avión LANSA Desaparecido el 24," *La Prensa*, Jan. 3, 1972.

"The jungle has swallowed the plane": "Muere Padre de Pasajero Cuandolba Por Noticia," *La Nueva Crónica*, Dec. 30, 1971.

Hercules plane on the way: "Hércules de Gran Autonomia de Vuelo Llega Para Buscar al LANSA Perdido," *La Prensa*, Jan. 4, 1972.

"It'll take a miracle": "El Milagro de Juliane," *Caretas*, Jan. 14, 1972.

"I'm a girl": Koepcke, *When I Fell*, 99. The original account in *Stern* has her saying, "There are dead people" and passing out: "Eine Kam Durch," *Stern*, Jan. 16, 1972.

Chapter 9: Survivor

From Juliane's encounter with the forest workers to her arrival at Yarinacocha is drawn from Koepcke, *When I Fell*, 101–105; Herzog, *Wings of Hope*; and "So habe ich überlebt," *Stern*, Feb. 6, 1972.

"It's a good thing": Koepcke, *When I Fell*, 101.

"What about the other passengers?": Koepcke, *When I Fell*, 102.

The pilot who flew Juliane to Yarinacocha was Jerrie Cobb, one of the first American women to pass screening tests to become an astronaut. When NASA refused to accept her and other women into the Mercury program, Cobb went to South America to fly as a missionary pilot.

Writing 40 years later, Juliane remembers being terrified on the plane ride. But according to *Stern*, she said, "I had no fear as I boarded": "So habe ich überlebt," *Stern*, Feb. 6, 1972.

Pat Davis and the Hedges children are profiled in "Lansa Accident and Search Report," *Translation*, April–June 1972, Wycliffe Bible Translators.

"Roberto! Roberto!": Author interview with Bob Weninger.

Weninger's discovery of the wreckage is from my interview with him and "The Twelve Days of Christmas 1971," *Aviation News*, Dec. 1972.

Juliane's reunion with her father is described in Koepcke, *When I Fell*, 117–119.

Chapter 10: The Story

Juliane describes the letters she received in Koepcke, *When I Fell*, 127–131.

"There are dead people!": "Eine Kam Durch," *Stern*, Jan. 16, 1972. This is from *Stern*'s first article, which is riddled with mistakes. They also claim that when Juliane woke up in the airplane seat on the forest floor, there were two corpses sitting next to her.

"Miracle in the jungle": "Alemana Sobrevivió Tras Caminar 9 Días en Selva," *La Nueva Crónica*, Jan. 5, 1972.

"a modern heroine": "Juliane Koepcke: Una Heroína Moderna," *La Nueva Crónica*, Jan. 7, 1972.

"coolheaded" and "fearless": Koepcke, *When I Fell*, 127.

Arrival of first seven victims: "La Fuerza Aérea Rescató los Restos Del Piloto Carlos Forno y de 6 Más," *La Prensa*, Jan. 9, 1972.

Patrols: "Patrulla Militar Va a Zona Del LANSA," *La Prensa*, Jan. 6, 1972.

Helicopter: "Hoy Queda Listo El Helipuerto Para el Rescate," *La Prensa*, Jan. 7, 1972.

"suitcases had opened in midair": Dr. Juan Zaplana Ramirez, in Herzog, *Wings of Hope*.

Ribeiro: "Hallan 40 Cadaveres En Restos del Avion," *La Prensa*, Jan. 9, 1972.

Half the bodies recovered: "46 Cadáveres Son Ubicados; Sigue Búsqueda," *La Prensa*, Jan. 10, 1972.

Identifying remains: "Traumatismos Causaron Muerte De Ocupantes de Avión LANSA," *La Prensa*, Jan. 10, 1972.

Cause of the crash is assessed in the accident report for LANSA Flight 508, International Civil Aviation Organization.

LANSA's negligence in the earlier crash is discussed in Herzog, *Wings of Hope*; and "Peruvian Line Suspended," *New York Times*, Sept. 4, 1970.

LANSA shut down for good: Koepcke, *When I Fell*, 148–149; and "Cancelan a la Cía. LANSA El Permiso de Operación," *La Prensa*, Jan. 5, 1972.

Juliane's return to Lima and to Germany is described in Koepcke, *When I Fell*, 148–153.

Epilogue: Payback

Juliane describes her recurring nightmares in Koepcke, *When I Fell*, 148.

"I cried for hours": "Sole Survivor: The Woman Who Fell to Earth," *The Telegraph*, March 22, 2012.

Juliane describes her time doing research at Panguana in Koepcke, *When I Fell*, 184–206.

"I took in the forest": Koepcke, *When I Fell*, 206.

"I felt as if I were plunging": Koepcke, *When I Fell*, 206.

"My task has a name": Koepcke, *When I Fell*, 206.

The account of the movie is drawn from Koepcke, *When I Fell*, 106–114; the movie itself, Herzog, *Wings of Hope*; and Cronin, *Herzog on Herzog*, 268–270.

"It's a mechanism": Koepcke, *When I Fell*, 113.

"Lying there like that": Koepcke, *When I Fell*, 113.

Lost nearly 15 percent of its trees: "Deforestation declines in the Amazon rainforest," Mongabay, Oct. 6, 2015. https://news.mongabay.com/2015/10/deforestation-declines-in-the-amazon-rainforest/

600 football fields an hour: "Calculating Deforestation Figures for the Amazon," Mongabay, Jan. 24, 2016. http://rainforests.mongabay.com/amazon/deforestation_calculations.html

100,000 miles of illegal roads: "Last of the Amazon," *National Geographic*, Jan. 2007.

Mahogany trade is discussed in "Mahogany logging in the Amazon," Global Forest Atlas, http://globalforestatlas.yale.edu/amazon/forests-and-logging/amazon-mahogany; and "Brazil: Mahogany loggers destroying the Amazon forest," World Rainforest Movement, http://wrm.org.uy/oldsite/bulletin/53/Brazil.html

Illegal mining in Peru is described in "Deforestation in Peru," *World Wildlife Magazine*, Fall 2015.

Extent of beef industry in the Amazon is discussed in "Cattle Ranching in the Amazon Region," Global Forest Atlas, http://globalforestatlas.yale.edu/amazon/land-use/cattle-ranching

2 million tons of beef: "Livestock and Poultry: World Markets and Trade," USDA, Oct. 2016.

"the railroad and the steamboat": quoted in Hemming, *Tree of Rivers*, 128.

Inefficiency of farming and ranching is discussed in "Project Amazonia: Threats—Agriculture and Cattle Ranching," from an M.I.T. research project, http://web.mit.edu/12.000/www/m2006/final/threats/threat_agg.html

The effect of deforestation on the environment is explained in "Deforestation," National Geographic, http://environment.nationalgeographic.com/environment/global-warming/deforestation-overview/

"As long as we regard": Koepcke, *When I Fell*, 157.

Juliane's memoir is built around her trip back to Peru to make Panguana a nature reserve. See especially 210–217.

"The Door": Koepcke, *When I Fell*, 109.

"In the city, nature is a guest": Koepcke, *When I Fell*, 157.

"I'm trying to save": "Sole Survivor: The Woman Who Fell to Earth," *The Telegraph*, March 22, 2012.

ACKNOWLEDGMENTS

It would feel strange not to thank Juliane Koepcke Diller, even though I never spoke with her. She has turned a tragedy into a life devoted to two vital causes: science and the rainforest. I can only hope she would find this book to be a faithful retelling of her story.

Thanks also to the people who shared their memories of the crash with me: Bob Weninger, Doug Deming, Ed Schertz, and Nicholas Asheshov. Bob Weninger passed away about a month after I spoke with him. He was eighty-six and had led a life of adventure and good works. I'm also grateful to Kevin Lyon, brother of Nathan Lyon, who generously supplied pictures of his brother and the Hedges family. In a poignant and perhaps hopeful postscript to this story, he and Rebecca Hedges, who lost her parents in the LANSA crash, married in 2001.

As always, research requires a ton of help. Jason Phillips of Wings of Hope and Brian Moyer of Wycliffe Bible Translators located articles and did their best to put me in touch with people whose lives were impacted by the LANSA crash. The staff at VCFA's Gary Library helped me dig up hard-to-find materials. Chris Schoop connected me to his people in Peru. Daniel Sáenz Santos photographed hundreds of newspaper articles at the National Library in Lima, and Daniel Matus helped me translate them.

Ideas don't develop in a vacuum. Elizabeth Ward and Shari Joffe introduced me to Juliane's story. Thanks also to friends and colleagues Marc Aronson, John Glenn, Lauren Tarshis, Leda Schubert, and Daphne Kalmar.

I'm grateful as always to Laura Williams McCaffrey for squeezing her indispensable critiques into her writing and teaching life. Mark Seidenfeld generously provided expert advice and counsel. Paige Hazzan at Scholastic continues to guide the LOST books artfully from idea to market. Miriam Altshuler guides me, which may be an even harder task and is probably above and beyond her job description as an agent.

Thanks, finally, to Estie, Richard, and Pat, who are LOST's biggest promoters; to Richard for his wise manuscript critiques; and to Jill, Zoë, and Finn for their encouragement, support, and forbearance.

ABOUT THE AUTHOR

TOD OLSON is the author of the historical fiction series How to Get Rich and the first two books in this series, *Lost in the Pacific, 1942* and *Lost in Outer Space*. He works as an editor, holds an MFA from Vermont College of Fine Arts, and lives in Vermont with his family, his mountain bike, and his electric reclining chair.

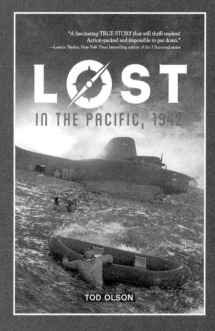
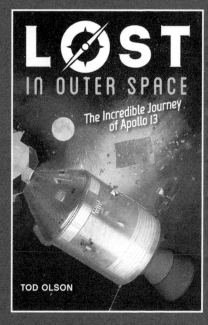